BEYOND
THE ORDINARY LEADER

PALMETTO
PUBLISHING
Charleston, SC
www.PalmettoPublishing.com

Copyright © 2024 by Lindsay M. Ellis

All rights reserved
No portion of this book may be reproduced, stored in a retrieval system, or transmitted in any form by any means—electronic, mechanical, photocopy, recording, or other—except for brief quotations in printed reviews, without prior permission of the author.

Paperback ISBN: 979-8-8229-5830-2
eBook ISBN: 979-8-8229-5831-9
Audiobook ISBN: 979-8-8229-5832-6

BEYOND
THE ORDINARY LEADER

*THE NO-SUCK
LEADERSHIP
MANIFESTO*

Lindsay M. Ellis

Contents

Dedication	1
Author's Note	3
Introduction - The Journey to No-Suck Leadership	7
Chapter 1 - Exploring Various Leadership Styles	11
Chapter 2 - Putting In The Work	25
Chapter 3 - Setting Exceptional Goals For Yourself and Your Team	36
Chapter 4 - Embracing Accountability - The Cornerstone of An Extraordinary Leader	45
Chapter 5 - Providing Impactful Guidance and Recognition	49
Chapter 6 - Leading, Mentoring, Coaching, and Managing	65
Chapter 7 - Harmonizing Work and Life: Strategies to Avoid Burnout	74
Chapter 8 - A Guide to Self-Care and Continuous Personal Growth	81
Chapter 9 - Things that Make You Go, Hmmm...	92
Chapter 10 - Leaving Your Leadership Legacy	97
Conclusion	102
Appendix	104
References	110
Testimonials	112

Dedication

This book is a tribute to my son, husband, and parents. Their unwavering support has been the foundation of this book. To my dad, thank you for being my business and life mentor! To my mom, thank you for always being my cheerleader, offering support, and being the first to tell me how proud you are of my accomplishments. Your belief in me as an author inspired me to write this book. To my husband, thank you for being my best friend and supporter and for always being there to listen and help. To my son, thank you for being my biggest cheerleader and my Why! I also want to express my gratitude to all my previous leaders and subordinates who have contributed to my growth as a leader. A special thanks to my CMO, Larisa, at Equity Lifestyle Properties, who believed in me and helped me to get to the next level in my career and become a great leader!

Author's Note

For the past two decades, I've been fully immersed in the marketing field, holding pivotal roles such as Marketing Coordinator at Centex Homes, Marketing and Sales Director at The Princeton Review, Director of Property Marketing at Equity Lifestyle Properties, Vice President of Marketing and Sales at Treehouse Communities, and Director of Marketing at Re-Bath, Wildflower, and FOR Energy. I've been a part of the executive leadership teams of Treehouse Communities, Wildflower, and FOR Energy, contributing to strategic decisions that extended beyond marketing. I've also led the reputation management departments at RE-Bath, Wildflower, and FOR Energy and initiated the culture committee at FOR Energy. But what truly fuels my passion is nurturing current and future leaders, a commitment that's evident in my three-year tenure teaching business and marketing courses at two universities.

I drew inspiration for this book from my observations of the many people leaving their jobs due to poor leadership. Ironically, I have personally experienced this, leaving several positions due to subpar leadership. However, those experiences taught me invaluable lessons about the kind of leader I did not want to become.

My Leadership Legacy

One of my core values has always been mentoring the teams under my leadership, ensuring their success by providing resources and maintaining an open-door policy. I take pride in the fact that many individuals I've led have moved on to achieve success in their careers. Hearing from them and knowing that I played a role in their journey is a tremendous compliment, as is the legacy I aim to leave when transitioning from a company. It is a legacy I hope my son will witness and carry forward.

One of my most gratifying achievements occurred during my tenure at Equity Lifestyle Properties, where I led a team. Under my guidance were two marketing specialists who had recently graduated from college and had no prior experience leading teams or working in marketing.

By the time I transitioned to a new role, both individuals had been promoted to managerial positions and were successfully leading their own teams. Witnessing their professional growth and their impact on the business was immensely rewarding. Not only did they excel in their roles, but they also cultivated teams that consistently met their goals and contributed to the company's growth trajectory. Even after my departure, I continue to receive calls from them seeking advice, a testament to the enduring impact of our collaboration and mentorship.

What Drives Me

My aspiration is not merely to be labeled as the best leader or to receive compliments. Instead, my focus is on making my team and the company I work for successful. Authenticity and sincerity are paramount to me. Leaders are on a lifelong journey of continuous training and growth, and I genuinely believe that. Leadership is a blend of innate qualities and skills honed through experience, constant learning, and drawing insights from others.

My journey as a leader traces back to my earliest years when I naturally gravitated towards guiding others, be it my stuffed animals, younger brother, or friends. As I matured, I found fulfilment in assisting others and guiding them toward solutions that brought them happiness and achievement.

My professional journey further solidified my commitment to moral leadership. I made a conscious vow never to replicate the poor leadership behaviors I experienced throughout my career. My mission is clear: to lead with integrity, empathy, and a steadfast dedication to the growth and well-being of those I have the privilege to lead.

"The function of leadership is to produce more leaders, not more followers."
~**Ralph Nader**

Introduction - The Journey to No-Suck Leadership

Are you a great leader? Or do you suck as a leader?

Extraordinary leaders make a positive and lasting impact on the organizations and employees they work with. But how does one become an extraordinary leader? Many people are born with inherent leadership traits; others have gained skills as they navigated their careers. However, leadership is a journey that takes forethought, introspection, and continuous learning. Great leaders employ all three as they advance through their careers. However, far too many leaders do the following:

- **Mistake leadership for micromanagement, where a leader closely observes, controls, or directs the work of their subordinates to an excessive degree, which:**
    - Stifles creativity and autonomy.
    - Demotivates.
    - Creates a culture of distrust.
    - Drives turnover.
- **Mistake leadership for friendship, which:**
    - Results in prioritizing being liked over providing direction and accountability.
    - Makes decisions based on personal feelings instead of what is best for the team and organization.

- - Causes a lack of boundaries between leaders and subordinates.
  - Compromises objective feedback.
- **Fear that their subordinates' success is a threat to their job, which:**
  - May result in leaders withholding opportunities for their subordinates' advancement.
  - Creates toxicity among the team.
  - Causes innovation and creativity to suffer.
  - Results in the organization losing out on leveraging its internal talent pool.

In many cases, people are promoted into leadership roles because they are proficient at their jobs rather than because they have leadership experience. Moreover, many current and aspiring leaders feel they are too busy or are not equipped with the skills needed to be extraordinary leaders who cultivate a successful career and team and help to positively impact an organization.

Consider this an example of poor leadership:

I started working for a new company. I was there only two weeks before I began to notice the red flags that caused so many Marketing Directors before me to leave (four in the last three years). As I sat in my office working through my list of tasks, all of a sudden, over the intercom for the whole office to hear, the company owner, my boss, calls me to come to the conference room to tell him what the f**** I was thinking when I made the flyer that I left on his desk to review. I was mortified. Why had he not just come to my office or called me directly?

I walked into the conference room to find out that I had designed an 8.5" x 11" flyer, and they had always done ½ page flyers, not the entire page like my flyer. This is an example of the type of behavior I categorize as sucking! This was a simple mistake that any new hire would have made had they not been given the proper expectations; you don't know what you don't know! In addition, a good leader would have walked into my office or talked to me one-on-one in the conference room and not used explicit language to make his point.

On the other hand, I had the privilege of working under an incredible visionary CMO at Equity Lifestyle Properties. She firmly believed in the power of sharing knowledge to enhance our team's success. Consequently, she held weekly team leader meetings where we discussed current projects and their status and addressed overarching issues. Each meeting served as a platform for collective knowledge-sharing and collaborative problem-solving. Whether the topic drove new business or resolved existing challenges, this practice fostered team buy-in, cooperation, and shared expertise.

This book will explore and provide the tools you need to achieve your greatest success as a leader. You will understand the importance of prioritizing people, culture, and growth. You will discover why mentoring and promoting those who work for you are crucial to your success. You will learn effective practices to keep your team motivated and focused on meeting their goals, and you will learn how to eliminate those practices that make a leader suck, contributing to the loss of critical employees.

While numerous leadership books teach greatness, this one takes a different approach by showing you how not to suck as a leader while becoming a leader that is beyond the ordinary. Understanding the characteristics of a terrible, uninspiring leader is critical to becoming a successful leader people want to work with. I have learned many lessons on what not to do from leaders who suck, and I want to provide you with a framework on how to advance beyond an ordinary leader.

Here is what I want you to take away from this book:

How to:
- Go beyond the ordinary and not suck as a leader.
- Motivate, inspire, and effectively mentor your team.

- Provide recognition and feedback that motivates.
- Understand the importance of putting in the effort required to be a great leader.
- Be a successful leader while cultivating successful leaders.
- Be a successful leader while not neglecting your personal growth.

Please note that this book is filled with anecdotes and stories illustrating leadership missteps. Shifting from merely seeing each tale as a depiction of a poor leader to actively recognizing our own tendencies to display similar behaviors will demand introspection and help you become a better leader.

Chapter 1 - Exploring Various Leadership Styles

Different Kinds of Leaders

As a successful leader who is more than just proficient in their skill area, you need to recognize that there are various leadership styles. Each style has its own set of strengths and weaknesses. It's crucial to understand that employees thrive under different types of leadership, often benefiting from a combination of styles.

Ineffective leaders often fail to recognize the significance of their leadership style. Some are rigidly held to one style. For example, some adopt a unilateral "boss" mentality, expecting unquestioning obedience. This one-sided approach frequently results in dissatisfaction among team members and contributes to a high turnover.

Let's look at an example from one of my previous jobs. I worked for a leader who hired me as a Director but had difficulty letting me utilize the years of experience I brought on board. His style was very transactional. He wanted me to use his content word for word on anything I created. Instead of allowing me to make changes, improve efficiency, or put a creative spin on the current processes, I just had to follow what had already been created. This put me in the position of a Marketing Coordinator, but I was not utilizing my talents that he had stated he was hiring me for.

I thrive on being a visionary who creates and implements strategy and new campaigns to grow businesses. I thrive on challenge and the ability to think creatively and autonomously.

Thus, the job was not as advertised and was not a fit for me, so after nine months, I ended up leaving for a position that I was better suited for.

In this case, my boss should have taken a really close look at what he wanted from the position and hired a marketing coordinator, or he should have realized that the job description demanded someone more tenured who would thrive under more autonomy and creative freedom.

Let's examine the multiple types of leaders:

1. **Transformational Leader**
    - Thrives on creating unity and ensures everyone moves in the same direction.
    - Aims to inspire and motivate their employees.
    - Seeks to help employees identify their strengths, overcome weaknesses, and grow within the organization.

    This is the most successfull style during periods of change or "transformation".

2. **Delegative Leader**
    - Thrives on assigning initiatives to employees.
    - Very hands-off.
    - Relies on and trusts their team.
    - Allows for significant autonomy and creativity.
    - Provides minimal feedback and guidance.

    This style flourishes with more established, competent employees but can be challenging to new hires.

3. **Authoritative Leader**
    - Employs a visionary approach, which is a clear and compelling vision for the future that inspires and motivates others to work toward that vision.

- Expects the team to follow their lead.
- Is motivational and inspiring.
- Very hands-on and provides much guidance.

This style is successful unless the leader micromanages, and then it is no longer motivational or inspiring.

4. **Transactional Leader**
    - Relies on organizational structure, which encompasses established guidelines, procedures, rewards, and consequences to regulate the actions and interactions of the team.
    - Establishes clear goals.
    - Establishes and communicates reward programs.
    - Defines responsibilities for each employee.
    - Prefers stability and is not a fan of organizational changes.

5. **Participative Leader**
    - Involves employees in all decisions.
    - Shares power and responsibility with the team.
    - Fosters trust between employees and leaders.

Although this style fosters trust and participation, it can be time-consuming and inefficient.

6. **Servant Leader**
    - Gets to know their team.
    - Makes decisions based on what is suitable for everyone involved.
    - Helps to develop and grow all members of their team.

This type of leadership results in increased loyalty, communication, and productivity, but like participative leadership, it can be time-consuming.

Discover Your Leadership Style Assessment

Understanding your leadership style is crucial in becoming a more effective leader. This assessment will help you identify your predominant leadership style and provide insights into your strengths and areas for development. Answer each question honestly and thoughtfully.

Section 1: Decision-Making

1. **In a challenging situation, I am more likely to:**
    a. Take charge and make decisions independently, focusing on the greater good.
    b. Gather input from team members before making a decision.
    c. Inspire and motivate others to collectively find a solution.
    d. Clearly define tasks and expectations for everyone.
    e. Provide space for the team to self-organize and make decisions.
    f. Focus on serving others, ensuring their needs are met.

Section 2: Collaboration

2. **When working on a project, I prefer:**
    a. Taking charge and leading the team.
    b. Facilitating group discussions and seeking input from everyone.
    c. Inspiring creativity and fostering a collaborative environment.
    d. Setting clear goals and monitoring progress.
    e. Allowing team members the freedom to work independently.

      f. Focusing on serving the needs of the team.

Section 3: Motivation
3. **I believe effective leadership involves:**
   a. Leading by example and making decisive moves.
   b. Empowering others by considering their opinions.
   c. Inspiring and motivating others toward a shared vision.
   d. Recognizing and rewarding individual achievements.
   e. Trusting the team's abilities and providing autonomy.
   f. Prioritizing the well-being and growth of team members.

Section 4: Task Management
4. **My approach to task completion is to:**
   a. Provide clear instructions and expect adherence.
   b. Collaboratively set goals and expectations.
   c. Encourage innovative solutions and flexibility.
   d. Monitor progress closely and adjust as needed.
   e. Delegate tasks and allow team members to take ownership.
   f. Focus on serving the needs of the team to achieve tasks.

Section 5: Hands-On Vs. Hands-Off Approach
5. **When faced with a challenge, I am inclined to:**
   a. Take control and guide the team through the solution.
   b. Facilitate open discussions and encourage team members to find solutions.
   c. Inspire creativity and let the team explore various approaches.

d. Provide clear instructions and let individuals complete tasks.
   e. Trust the team's abilities and allow them to handle challenges independently.
   f. Serve the team by providing support and resources to overcome challenges.

Section 6: Communication
6. **When communicating with your team, do you:**
   a. Provide clear instructions and expectations, ensuring everyone understands their roles.
   b. Encourage open dialogue and active listening, valuing input from all team members.
   c. Inspire and motivate through storytelling and visionary messages.
   d. Provide regular updates and feedback, focusing on accountability and performance.
   e. Trust your team to communicate amongst themselves, intervening only when necessary.
   f. Focus on empathy and understanding, ensuring everyone feels heard and valued.

Section 7: Conflict Resolution
7. **How do you typically approach conflict within your team?**
   a. Address issues directly, providing solutions and guidance as needed.
   b. Facilitate open discussions, allowing all parties to express their perspectives and work towards a resolution together.
   c. Inspire reconciliation and understanding, guiding the team towards a mutually beneficial outcome.
   d. Set clear boundaries and consequences, ensuring accountability and adherence to protocols.

e. Delegate conflict resolution tasks to the involved parties, stepping in only if necessary.

f. Prioritize empathy and compromise, fostering a supportive environment for conflict resolution.

Section 8: Decision-Making
8. **When faced with a major decision, how do you typically approach it?**

   a. Make decisions swiftly, considering the overall impact on the organization or project.

   b. Seek input from relevant stakeholders, ensuring diverse perspectives are considered before reaching a conclusion.

   c. Inspire creativity and innovation, encouraging the exploration of unconventional solutions.

   d. Base decisions on established protocols and past successes, focusing on efficiency and consistency.

   e. Delegate decision-making authority to capable team members, trusting their judgment and expertise.

   f. Prioritize the well-being and values of the team when making decisions, seeking solutions that align with their needs.

Scoring:
- **Count the number of each letter you selected.**
- **The category with the highest count is likely your predominant leadership style.**

Interpretation:
   A. Authoritative Leader.
   B. Participative Leader.
   C. Transformational Leader.
   D. Transactional Leader.

E. Delegative Leader.
F. Servant Leader.

Interpreting Your Score
Authoritative Leader (A):
- **Likely Traits:**
    - Decisive.
    - Confident.
    - Assertive.
- **Strengths:**
    - Effective in crisis situations.
    - Able to provide clear direction.
- **Areas for Development:**
    - May overlook input from others, which can be very disengaging.
- **Guidance:**
    - Practice being an active listener.
    - Foster collaboration by seeking input from team members.
    - Use more inclusive decision-making by being open to multiple viewpoints.

Participative Leader (B):
- **Likely Traits:**
    - Democratic.
    - Collaborative.
    - Inclusive.
- **Strengths:**
    - Foster a sense of ownership among the team.
- **Areas for Development:**
    - The decision-making process may be time-consuming in urgent situations.
- **Guidance:**
    - Prioritize team involvement.

- o Streamline processes for increased efficiency.
- o Ensure clear communication to prevent decision paralysis.

Transformational Leader (C):
- **Likely Traits:**
    - o Visionary.
    - o Inspirational.
    - o Motivational.
- **Strengths:**
    - o Inspire innovation and creativity.
    - o Drive organizational change.
- **Areas for Development:**
    - o May need help with detailed implementation and to maintain focus on short-term goals.
- **Guidance:**
    - o Collaborate with transactional leaders to ensure effective execution of ideas.
    - o Develop strategies to balance long-term vision with short-term objectives.

Transactional Leader (D):
- **Likely Traits:**
    - o Structured.
    - o Goal-oriented.
    - o Rewards-driven.
- **Strengths:**
    - o Ensure accountability and efficiency in task completion.
- **Areas for Development:**
    - o Potential to stifle creativity and innovation in favor of adherence to protocols.
- **Guidance:**

- Encourage a culture of innovation by allowing for experimentation within established frameworks.
- Recognize and reward creativity and initiative alongside adherence to protocols.

Delegative Leader (E):
- **Likely Traits:**
    - Trusting.
    - Hands-off.
    - Empowering.
- **Strengths:**
    - Foster autonomy and development among team members.
- **Areas for Development:**
    - Risk of detachment from team activities, leading to lack of oversight.
- **Guidance:**
    - Maintain regular check-ins to stay informed about team progress and provide support as needed.
    - Clarify expectations and boundaries to ensure accountability despite delegating authority.

Servant Leader (F):
- **Likely Traits:**
    - Selfless.
    - Empathetic.
    - Supportive.
- **Strengths:**
    - Build strong relationships and foster a supportive work environment.
- **Areas for Development:**
    - May prioritize team needs at the expense of organizational goals.

- **Guidance:**
    - Maintain a balance between individual support and organizational objectives.
    - Communicate the importance of aligning personal and team goals with broader organizational vision.

No matter how you score on the assessment, the most successful leaders understand their team members, how they work best, and the company's vision and goals. There is no one-size-fits-all approach. While few people thrive under micromanagement, some need more guidance and support than others. Similarly, only a few succeed under an absentee leader, but some require more autonomy than others.

Though I lean towards participative leadership, relying solely on one leadership style is a misconception. I've led individuals who benefit from a more authoritative approach, especially those starting their careers and seeking guidance. Additionally, incorporating elements of transactional leadership across teams ensures accountability and goal attainment while providing a framework for rewards and consequences.

Recently, we taught our son how to tie his shoes. Tying shoelaces is an essential life skill that my son needed to learn, especially since many of his friends already know how. Yet, with so many other activities he would rather do, we needed to find a way to motivate him. We decided that he could only play his video games once he learned how to tie his shoes. This motivation proved effective, but the key was varying our instructional approaches. We decided the three approaches below could be beneficial:

1. Show him a few times and say go and practice.
    a. This is Authoritative Leadership, as my husband and I take charge and demonstrate the skill, then have our son learn through independent practice.
2. Take his hands and guide him through the process.

    a. This is Participative Leadership, as my husband and I are actively involved in the process, providing hands-on support and guidance.
3. Have him take one shoe, and I take another, and we tie them simultaneously.
    a. This is Delegative Leadership, as my husband and I are empowering our son to take ownership of his learning while providing parallel guidance and participation.

We opted for all three approaches. We began by showing him, then guiding his hands, and finally, each of us had a shoe that we tied together. This combination of styles allowed him to learn quickly. We had him practice nightly to reinforce the learning, celebrating each successful tie.

Navigating this teaching journey, we acknowledged that there's no manual for raising children. Yet, leveraging our understanding of our son's needs and our expertise in the task at hand, we devised what we deemed the most effective plan. Should obstacles have arisen, we were prepared to reassess and refine our approach accordingly.

This experience underscores the significance of tailoring approaches to individual needs, fostering diverse strategies for effective learning and growth. Furthermore, it emphasizes the importance of providing guidance, feedback, and recognition, topics we'll delve into later in this book.

Supporting Your Team

"A true leader has the confidence to stand alone, the courage to make tough decisions, and the compassion to listen to the needs of others."
                                                            ~Douglas MacArthur

While it is essential to have leaders who are experts in their craft, when hiring or promoting an employee to a leadership position, the focus should be on identifying individuals with the traits necessary to be successful. When evaluating candidates for promotion, particularly first-time leaders, organizations must recognize and assess the candidate's leadership styles, skills, and abilities to ensure success in their new role. Moreover, all leaders should receive training and resources to enhance their leadership capabilities.

One frequently overlooked trait, yet crucial for a team's success, is the ability to advocate for the team's ideas, speak up when necessary, and defend team members when warranted. This most closely aligns with Servant Leadership. While being a "yes" person may gain favor with upper management, it often results in decreased morale and employee attrition. To avoid this pitfall and not suck as a leader, it's imperative to have a backbone and be confident. This does not mean opposing every idea from upper management; instead, it emphasizes the importance of speaking up when warranted.

In a previous role, my boss, the Chief Marketing Officer (CMO), had never led people or worked in a team setting before coming to the company. Our CEO would assign tasks to her, which she then delegated to our team. These tasks consumed a significant amount of time. Unfortunately, when presenting the completed projects to the CEO, her misunderstanding of his instructions often led to substantial criticism. Instead of advocating for the team or seeking additional guidance, she apologized for perceived errors and mandated that we redo the projects.

One such instance was when she tasked me with completely revamping the referral program from start to finish. She requested flow charts for each step and a draft training manual, providing all the necessary calculations and guidelines. Once I finished the charts and manual, she approved them. However, when she presented the finished product to the CEO, it resulted in me having to completely redo the entire project five times over three months. The issues mainly stemmed from discrepancies in the calculations and plan implementation, differing from the CEO's expectations.

This not only proved frustrating but also far from cost-effective.

In a leadership role, it is imperative to have the courage to voice concerns or seek clarification to prevent such counterproductive and exasperating scenarios. Ideally, she should have ensured a clear understanding of the CEO's expectations. In instances where clarity was lacking, she should have sought clarification. Alternatively, if she believed the team had met the requirements, she should have defended the team and explained why she thought they had fulfilled the CEO's request.

Exceptional leaders exhibit ease in seeking clarification and adeptly defending their teams while challenging established norms. Organizations seek leaders who contribute to the company's overall value and boldly voice innovative ideas while scrutinizing those that may not prove advantageous.

> "A good leader takes a little more than his share of the blame, a little less than his share of the credit."
> ~**Arnold H. Glasow**

In Summary

In the vast leadership landscape, we have reviewed each leadership style, its strengths, areas for development, and guidance on how to use them successfully. Acknowledging that employees thrive under various leadership approaches, the path to extraordinary leadership requires a nuanced understanding and a willingness to blend styles as needed. An ordinary leader stays in their lane, keeping to their dominant style, while the extraordinary leader can use elements of each.

The leadership style assessment should serve as a compass, guiding us to understand our predominant leadership approach. Whether authoritative, participative, transformational, transactional, delegative, or servant, the key lies in defining our style and embodying its essence with authenticity and adaptability.

Chapter 2 - Putting In The Work

In the hustle and bustle of daily life, it is easy to succumb to the notion that time is a scarce commodity. After a while, this becomes an excuse to refrain from investing effort into activities that will prove most beneficial to you and your team or family in the long run.

Let's revisit my story about teaching my son to tie his shoes. We could have given in to the dual pressures of his lack of motivation and our busy schedules, opting to continue to buy him Velcro shoes. While this might have provided immediate relief, it would have been a short-sighted decision. In the long run, he would have faced ridicule, and we would still be tying his shoes long after he outgrew the convenience of Velcro.

Taking the time to impart this essential life skill to our son meant more than just avoiding embarrassment; it meant ensuring he could keep up with his peers, wear any shoe style, and granted us extra time during hectic moments. Despite the busyness surrounding us, investing time in essential tasks pays off in the form of long-term benefits for individuals and their support systems.

Put In the Work

"The only place where success comes before work is in the dictionary."
~Vidal Sassoon

There has never been a great leader who hires a staff member and then throws them to the wolves with no training. To set your team and thus yourself up for success, you must invest the necessary time and work in the beginning when it comes to people, resources, and processes. Even if you hire an employee with years of experience, they will need to gain the knowledge of your organization.

Resources

There are some essential resources to have in place to set your team up for success. These include:

- Drafted roles and responsibilities for each position.
- Service Level Agreements (SLA).
- Standard Operating Procedures (SOP).
- Training Guides/Manuals.

Let us address the importance of each one individually.

All employees from the top down should have a clearly written list of roles and responsibilities. This practice facilitates better recruitment by enabling companies to attract candidates ideally suited for each role and ensures role clarity for existing employees, eliminating confusion about their job responsibilities. As a result, there will be heightened productivity, loyalty, job satisfaction, and overall effectiveness. According to a study done by Effectory, a consulting firm in the Netherlands, when people have a clear understanding of their roles and responsibilities, it leads to 53% more efficiency, a 27% boost in effectiveness, and a remarkable 25% increase in performance overall[1].

While a written list of roles and responsibilities is vital for the employee, it also serves as a roadmap for management

---

[1] Ninety. (2024). Defining Roles and Responsibilities Drives Team Productivity: https://www.ninety.io/blog/defining-roles-and-responsibilities#:~:text=Here%E2%80%99s%20what%20defining%20roles%20and%20responsibilities%20in%20a,key%20action.%20...%204%20Communication%20flows%20better.%20

in developing Standard Operating Procedures (SOPs), training programs, and goal setting. A proficient leader invests the time and effort required to effectively articulate each position's roles and responsibilities.

SLAs

Similar to roles and responsibilities, thoughtfully articulated service level agreements (SLAs) are important. While many organizations have SLAs in place for external vendors and customers, it is equally important to establish them internally within the company. SLAs outline the level of service among various departments within an organization. These documents should include a scope of service, performance standards, and clearly defined roles and responsibilities.

Let's take a New Home Builder as an example. SLAs should be written for:

- **CEO's Service to:**
    - The Executives.
    - The Employees.
    - The Company as a whole.
    - The Shareholders.
- **Marketing's Service to Sales**
- **Sales Service to:**
    - The Company.
    - Construction.
    - Home Buyers.
- **Accounting's Service to:**
    - Sales.
    - Home Buyers.
    - The Company as a whole.
- **Procurement/Purchasing Service to:**
    - Sales.
    - Home Buyers.
    - Construction.

- **Land Development's Service to:**
    - The Company.
    - Home Buyer.
    - Sales.

Let's draft the SLA for how Marketing supports Sales at a fictitious company, ABC Homes.

Service Scope
- Marketing will provide comprehensive support to the sales team at ABC Homes.
- Services include lead generation, collateral development, digital marketing, and promotional activities.

Lead Generation
- Marketing commits to generating a minimum of 100 qualified monthly leads for the sales team.
- Leads will be segmented and scored based on criteria established in collaboration with the sales team.

Collateral Development
- Marketing will produce high-quality brochures, flyers, and other promotional materials for all residential projects within two weeks of project launch.
- Sales-specific materials, such as pitch decks and presentation templates, will be updated and delivered within five business days of the sales team requesting changes.

Service Scope
- Marketing will maintain an active online presence, regularly updating the company website and social media platforms.
- Marketing will send monthly email campaigns to nurture leads and promote current offerings.

Events and Promotions

- Marketing will organize at least two quarterly promotional events to drive foot traffic and generate interest in ABC Homes.
- Marketing will participate in industry trade shows and coordinate local events to enhance brand visibility.

Reporting and Communication
- The sales team will receive a monthly report detailing lead generation, marketing activities, and performance metrics by the fifth business day of the following month.
- Schedule regular meetings to discuss ongoing campaigns, feedback, and upcoming initiatives.

Collaboration and Feedback
- Marketing and sales teams will meet bi-weekly to discuss ongoing projects, share insights, and address concerns.
- Marketing will actively seek feedback from the sales team to improve support services continuously.

Escalation Procedures
- If any issues impact sales support, a designated point of contact from both marketing and sales will convene to resolve the matter within 48 hours.

Performance Evaluation
- Quarterly reviews will be conducted to assess the effectiveness of marketing efforts in supporting sales goals.
- Make SLA adjustments collaboratively based on performance evaluations.

Exercise

Take a few minutes to draft a service-level agreement for your position at work or home. If you use your role at home, you can choose your SLA for your children, spouse, or roommate.

SOPs

While having clear roles and responsibilities and SLAs are crucial to a business and its leaders' success, Standard Operating Procedures (SOPs) also play a pivotal role. These detailed instructions, protocols, and guidelines outline the procedures required to complete the organization's tasks and processes. They encompass step-by-step instructions on fulfilling responsibilities, adhering to safety protocols, meeting documentation requirements, and utilizing relevant references.

For example, the SOPs for an outbound call center engaged in cold calling could encompass the following:

- Call Script.
- Number of Expected Daily Dials.
- Systems to be utilized.
- Procedure for documenting calls in the system/CRM.
- Feedback Process.
- Disciplinary Measures for Non-Compliance with SOPs.

All employees should receive their SOPs and sign off on them. This will ensure adherence and layout clear job expectations. SOPs should be reviewed annually and updated based on whether they have been effective and are current.

Training Guide

Last, a well-thought-out training guide is one of the most crucial yet often overlooked resources. It should be meticulously outlined and drafted, making it a mandatory resource for all employees. This guide should be distinct from an employee handbook, which highlights company rules and procedures. The training guide should provide comprehensive instructions for employees to fulfill their responsibilities successfully. New employees should receive a copy in hard format or digital, allowing them to refer back to the training anytime.

When creating training materials, aim for thought-provoking and interactive content. The more engaging and interactive the training, the better it captures the trainee's attention. While various digital software programs offer accessible platforms for creating fun training, you don't necessarily need special software. PowerPoint, Google Slides, Google Forms, or Word can be effective. The key is incorporating quizzes, surveys, and discussion questions to enhance engagement.

Here are some helpful steps when drafting a training manual:

1. Clearly outline the manual's objectives, keeping in mind what you want employees to achieve through the training.
2. Understand your audience and tailor the content to meet their needs.
3. Organize the information logically with a clear structure, using bullet points, headings, and subheadings for easier readability and quick reference.
4. Use clear and concise language, and avoid excessive technical terms or jargon.
5. Incorporate visual elements such as charts, diagrams, and images.
6. Break down all elements into clear step-by-step instructions.
7. Provide relatable and practical examples to enhance understanding.
8. Make it interactive with discussion questions, surveys, and quizzes.

9. Maintain consistent formatting throughout for a cohesive look and easier readability.
10. Regularly update the manual to reflect changes and ensure accuracy.

Does this sound like a lot of work? Are you too busy to do this? Yes, this can be a lengthy process, but it takes a lot more time to have a team that needs help understanding how to do their jobs, and you have to keep training over and over. Put in the effort in the beginning, and you will have a resource that makes that entire training process more efficient and successful, thus creating more time for you to do your job.

To streamline and simplify the process, you should define whose job it is to create the SLAs, SOPs, and training guides. Your department heads should be the ones to create these for each department, as they are the subject matter experts. However, the importance of these cannot be downplayed, so having department heads create them is just the first step. Human Resources and Executive Leadership should review and approve all SOPs and SLAs, and the Executive Leader of each department, in conjunction with the training department, should approve the training guides. To save time, HR and the Executives should set aside a day to review the SLAs and SOPs as a group. They should also review these annually or if changes are made.

Once you have the right resources drafted, you must have a solid plan to implement them. This plan should include:

- Onboarding process
    - Consider which documents need to be in this phase. This will be applicable to all new hires.
- Training program and schedule
    - Here is where the training guides come into play. Each department head should have a schedule based on the time it will take to learn the items in the guide.

- Milestones
    - Department heads should establish goals and timelines for mastery of each skill and plan for additional training if employees are not reaching their milestones.
- Feedback schedule
    - The department manager will conduct this, and it should be based on the length of training.

Recruiting, onboarding, and training demand significant time and resources. Therefore, you want to ensure that when you hire a new employee, you have all the processes to onboard them successfully. Comprehensive planning is necessary, covering every detail from paperwork completion and office tours to equipment setup and providing the required office supplies. It is essential to consider all the departments that will need to be involved, such as Human Resources, IT, and Marketing.

One exceptional onboarding experience I encountered was at a bathroom remodeling company. This company owned 102 franchises and had about fifty employees working at the office headquarters. They hired me to be the Marketing Director.

Upon arrival, I was directed to my office, where all of my equipment awaited me. A thoughtful gift bag, a backpack stocked with office supplies, a warm welcome card from the entire staff, and an agenda for the first week were waiting. The agenda included scheduled sessions with Human Resources for paperwork, an informative office tour, a meeting with IT to set up equipment, dedicated time with each department to understand their roles, a team lunch, a managerial lunch, and training sessions with my team and boss. This comprehensive onboarding approach, led by the training and development department in conjunction with Human Resources, IT, and Marketing, significantly eased my new employee nerves, fostering a genuine sense of welcome.

When it comes to implementing the training program and schedule, a practical approach is the development of a 30-day, 60-day, and 90-day plan. Each phase should encompass a unique set of initiatives the employee needs to learn and complete. This includes reviewing and mastering sections of the manual, engaging in on-the-job training, and participating in relevant projects. The overarching goal is for the employee to be fully functional by the end of the 90 days.

While having a plan is crucial, its success hinges on regular weekly check-in meetings to discuss progress and address any questions. Additionally, a feedback meeting at the end of each month provides an opportunity to assess overall performance. It is important to note that a 90-day plan may only be suitable for some roles; some may require shorter training periods, while others may necessitate longer durations. For instance, a new receptionist may need less training than someone who manufactures products. Therefore, tailor the plan to align with the specific training needs of the position.

I have observed far too many leaders who do not recognize the value of a structured training program and schedule. Some believe it consumes too much time, assuming employees will learn adequately as they progress. This is a fallacy. Failure to invest time in training new hires from the beginning may result in spending more time on training in the long run or even on training their replacement if they feel unsupported or lack clarity on how to perform their job.

An excellent example of this was at a previous job, where we had a team of brand ambassadors who went to events and booked appointments. We were attending so many events that the Event Manager needed additional support. Thus, she promoted her top performing Brand Ambassador to a lead position, which meant she did not have to attend every event, schedule the staff and manage all of the event supplies. This lead position meant that she could concentrate on new business opportunities instead of being bogged down by going to all the events. This also allowed her to promote our most passionate Brand Ambassador and give him a substantial raise. They were both excited at first. The excitement started to dwindle as she felt he was not doing his job and she was having to step in. He was frustrated because he did not know what was expected of him. Sure, she verbally articulated what she wanted the position to entail, but there was no training guide, goals, SOPs, or an SLA. Ultimately, he ended up leaving the company.

It is beneficial to shift your mindset towards recognizing the importance of a well-designed training manual and program. Investing time in this upfront effort can transform you into a leader for whom people actively want to work.

"The only thing worse than training employees and losing them is not training them and keeping them."

~Zig Ziglar

In Summary

In conclusion, effective leadership demands a commitment to investing time and effort into proactively developing comprehensive resources. While the initial workload may seem daunting, the long-term benefits far outweigh the investment. By prioritizing training and development, leaders can cultivate a motivated and skilled workforce, driving organizational success. Let us embrace the ethos of continuous improvement and invest in the growth and development of our teams. Take some time to evaluate the processes you have in place for your team.

Chapter 3 - Setting Exceptional Goals For Yourself and Your Team

A friend of mine started a new job. She was excited to apply her experience and education to help the business. The first week was filled with meet and greets, paperwork, and general onboarding. However, the second and third weeks were consumed by boredom, as her boss was too busy to train her or give her projects to do. She had already finished her assigned online company training, and being so new, she had no idea what to do next. Finally, at the end of week three, she met with her boss, who apologized for being so busy and gave her some tasks to complete. However, she was never given clear guidelines, goals, and job responsibilities. So, while she was great at being a task manager, she was left without a clear purpose and a lot of frustration. In addition, she would often turn in projects that would have to be revised as she was not given clear guidance. She tried to talk to her boss but was still not given the clarity she needed, so she found a new job.

Have you ever worked at a job without a clear sense of direction? This poses several challenges. When employees lack defined goals and performance standards, they often find themselves unchallenged and lacking motivation, and the company's productivity may fall short of the leaders' expectations.

But what exactly is a goal? A goal is a measurable outcome set to be achieved within a specified timeframe. Goals can range from short to long-term and play a fundamental role in planning and achieving success in both personal and professional contexts. To drive action effectively, goals must be meaningful and achievable. This requires a thoughtful and systematic approach, best achieved through setting S.M.A.R.T goals—goals that are:

- S = Specific.
- M = Measurable.
- A = Achievable.
- R = Relevant.
- T = Timely.

I learned this concept while pursuing my undergraduate degree and I have taken it to all my jobs. Additionally, many companies I worked for will train on setting S.M.A.R.T. goals.

Let's break down each component using the example of losing 10 pounds:

Specific: *Clearly define the goal.*
Example: "I want to lose 10 pounds in the next four months by exercising and maintaining a balanced diet."

Measurable: *Define how you will measure progress.*
Example: "I will step on the scale every Monday morning to track my progress."

Achievable: *Ensure the goal is attainable and realistic.*
Example: "I commit to exercising three times a week for thirty minutes, gradually increasing intensity and duration over the four months."

Relevant: *Verify that the goal matters to you.*
Example: "Losing 10 pounds aligns with my goal of looking and feeling better in my clothes."

Timely: *Set a deadline; introduce a sense of urgency.*
Example: "I will lose 10 pounds in four months."

Setting S.M.A.R.T. goals is just the beginning. To ensure success, document the goal, create an action plan, regularly review progress, and make adjustments when necessary. Setting milestones and celebrating achievements along the way can also enhance motivation. It is important to note that sometimes company and personal priorities change, or challenges arise; thus, it is essential to adjust the goal accordingly. For example, if I have a goal of having new tradeshow displays designed and printed this quarter, but my printer will not be able to meet the deadline, I either need to find a new printer or adjust the timely aspect of the goal.

As a leader, setting goals with team members, reviewing progress, and holding them accountable are crucial for goal attainment. In all of my jobs as a Marketing Director, at the end of each quarter, I would meet with each employee on my team to draft the next quarter's goals.

We did this collaboratively so there was buy-in from the employee and myself, and we knew the goals aligned with overall company goals and vision. Monthly check-ins followed, where we reviewed the goals, provided feedback, and made adjustments as needed. Encouraging employees to set both business and personal goals fosters a more holistic investment in each team member, valuing them as employees and individuals.

A great example of this is when I worked at Equity Lifestyle Properties. During the last week of each quarter, I would meet with all of my subordinates and discuss the previous quarter's goals, what had been completed, what hadn't, and why. Then, we would set the next quarter's goals. I would have them come prepared to suggest three to four business goals and one to two personal goals they wanted and felt they could accomplish in the next three months.

We would go through each goal by applying the S.M.A.R.T method, and once approved, these would serve as the framework for the larger projects that needed to be completed over the next quarter. We would then meet during the last week of each month to discuss progress toward the goal and challenges. This approach provided guidelines and support to each employee for what needed to be accomplished.

Vision Boards

It is not only essential for your employees to have goals; you, too, need goals. Creating a vision board is an excellent method to establish goals while providing a visual reminder for motivation. This can also be a fun exercise to conduct with your team.

A vision board visually represents one's goals, dreams, aspirations, and desires. It typically consists of a collage of images, words, phrases, and affirmations that reflect what a person wants to manifest or achieve. Vision boards are created with the intention of serving as a daily reminder of one's objectives. They can include various aspects of life, such as career, relationships, health, travel, personal development, and more. Creating a vision board often involves selecting images and words that resonate with the individual's desires and arranging them on a board or poster in a creative and inspiring way. The idea behind a vision board is that by regularly visualizing and focusing on these goals, individuals can increase their motivation, clarity, and determination to turn their dreams into reality.

"A TD Bank survey[2] found that one in five successful entrepreneurs use vision boards when starting their business, and about 76% reported that their progress so far has aligned with their vision. 82% of these small business owners found that they have accomplished over half of their business goals since they began."[3]

Let's get motivated by making a Vision Board:
1. Choose a format:

---

[2] PR Newswire. (2016). Visualizing Goals Influences Financial Health and Happiness, Study Finds: https://www.prnewswire.com/news-releases/visualizing-goals-influences-financial-health-and-happiness-study-finds-300207028.html

[3] Forbes. (2024). A Psychologist Explains The Power Of 'Vision Boarding' For Success. https://www.forbes.com/sites/traversmark/2024/03/29/a-psychologist-explains-the-power-of-vision-boarding-for-success/?sh=6b62100e4e69

a. Decide if you want your vision to board to be a collage of images, words, symbols, or a combination of them all.
2. Gather materials:
   a. Magazines, newspapers, or printed images.
   b. Scissors.
   c. Glue.
   d. Tape.
   e. Markers, crayons, colored pencils or pens.
3. Draft your goals:
   a. Take some time to draft both your personal and professional goals.
      i. Consider what brings you joy and fulfillment.
      ii. Engage in creative and reflective thinking.
      iii. Take some time to sit in a quiet place and visualize your aspirations and goals and how you would depict them visually.
4. Design your board:
   a. As you design your vision board, get creative and aspirational, expressing your goals visually.
      i. Remember, this is your "dream" board. It is what you want to accomplish in your life. Do not limit yourself and set boundaries. Your board can be as large or small as you desire and contain as many words and images as applicable.
5. Team exercise:
   a. If conducting this as a team exercise, have everyone present their completed vision boards.
   b. It would be helpful to have the leader present first or even present before assigning the team to design their boards.

c. Encourage team members to share the significance of each element on their boards.
6. Create an action plan:
   a. On a separate piece of paper or index card, formulate an action plan outlining steps to achieve the goals illustrated on your vision board.
7. Monthly check-ins:
   a. On a separate piece of paper or index card, formulate an action plan outlining steps to achieve the goals illustrated on your vision board.

Note: Vision boards are often filled with long-term goals due to their inspirational nature. However, whether long or short-term, goals should be achievable and timely. You do not have to be an artist. It does not have to look good; it just needs to depict your aspirations and goals. To see an example of a vision board, visit Appendix C.

This vision board exercise serves as a motivational tool and facilitates goal-setting in a creative and engaging manner. It encourages individuals and teams to envision their aspirations and develop actionable plans for success.

Goal Completion and Accountability Exercise

Here is another impactful exercise for a team or company to set and hold people accountable to their goals:

1. Give everyone a piece of paper and a quick paper airplane-making tutorial. YouTube has a lot of quick tutorials if needed.
2. Have everyone write one personal and one work goal as well as their name on the piece of paper and then make it into a paper airplane.
3. Have the team stand in a line and then, on the count of three, launch their planes.
4. Once all the planes have landed, each person should pick up a plane.

5. Each person is to read the goal on the plane and to hold the person accountable to that goal by checking in with them regularly on their progress, thus acting as their accountability coach.
6. Even the leaders should be involved.

Company Vision and Goals

In my experience working with an organization, we encountered significant hurdles in achieving our one and three-year vision initiatives. Upon reflection, it became clear that the root cause of our struggles lay in a lack of widespread communication regarding the company's vision, compounded by quarterly department goals that were not aligned with our overarching objectives.

The process began with the Executive Team convening for multiple days to meticulously draft the company's short-term (one-year) and longer-term (three-year) goals. These goals were diligently recorded within an accountability software system utilized by the organization, with annual reviews conducted by the Executive Team.

However, the disconnect emerged at the departmental level, where each Executive, Department Head, and employee set quarterly goals without adequate alignment with the company's overarching vision. Although progress on these quarterly goals was discussed in weekly manager meetings, the focus remained narrow, failing to account for the broader strategic objectives.

The consequences of this misalignment became painfully evident during an executive meeting, where cash flow issues were under scrutiny. Upon comparing quarterly goals against the one and three-year company objectives, it became apparent that we had veered off course, jeopardizing our financial targets by over a million dollars. With the three-year mark looming just two months away, the urgency to correct our course was palpable.

The repercussions of our oversight were severe. The decline in cash flow necessitated the closure of a department and regretfully resulted in the layoff of several employees. Furthermore, the organization underwent four business model changes within 18 months, reflecting the tumultuous consequences of our lack of strategic alignment.

This experience serves as a stark reminder of the dangers of insufficient role and goal clarity within an organization. Our struggles could have been mitigated through effective communication of the vision, initiatives, and overarching goals to all levels of the organization. Regular progress reviews would have facilitated early identification of misalignments, enabling prompt corrective action.

In hindsight, it is evident that adherence to our one and three-year goals could have provided much-needed guidance amidst the turbulence of constant change. As we move forward, we are committed to fostering a culture of alignment and accountability, ensuring that our goals reflect our collective vision for success.

Let's consider a personal example. Suppose you aspire to participate in the Disneyland Half Marathon next January, a goal set twelve months in advance despite never having run a half marathon before. To achieve this, you committed to running five days per week and increasing your distance by a mile each month, starting with one mile.

Let's imagine that you initially adhered to the plan by running five days per week but, due to other commitments, later reduced it to three days per week. Additionally, despite allocating an hour for running, you find that, by the end of the twelve months, you have only practiced running six miles, indicating that you are not adequately trained or prepared for the half marathon.

To ensure you met your established goal, there are several steps you could have taken:

Clearly write your S.M.A.R.T goal:

Clearly defining your Specific, Measurable, Achievable, Relevant, and Time-bound goal would have provided a roadmap for your training, making it easier to track and adhere to.

Set a monthly calendar reminder:

Establishing a routine of monthly reminders to increase your distance and review your progress could have helped you stay on track and make necessary adjustments.

Revised the goal when time was an issue:

Recognizing time constraints and revising your goal accordingly would have been a proactive approach. This might involve running longer distances on the three days you were able to allocate for running, ensuring that you still progress toward your goal despite a reduced frequency.

Chapter 4 - Embracing Accountability - The Cornerstone of An Extraordinary Leader

"The price of greatness is responsibility."
~Winston Churchill

While we have previously discussed responsibilities and goals, accountability goes a step further—it involves ensuring that those goals and responsibilities are completed as assigned by the responsible individuals. Holding people accountable is crucial to conveying the importance of fulfilling assigned tasks. Individuals should also embrace personal accountability for completing their tasks and achieving their goals. When mistakes occur, it is essential to acknowledge them, take responsibility, and rectify the situation.

What are the benefits of accountability?

Increased commitment to the job.
It often fosters a heightened commitment to completing tasks and achieving job responsibilities.

Increased job satisfaction.
Employees who take ownership of their work and tasks get projects to the finish line, leading to increased job satisfaction.

Improved work performance.
Employees take ownership of their jobs and strive to do their best.

While personal accountability and accountability for one's job are essential, the accountability demonstrated by leaders is pivotal. When leaders take accountability for their actions and responsibilities, they:

Set an example.
Leaders who hold themselves accountable set a compelling example for their team members. They showcase a commitment to the organization's success and emphasize the value they place on the team's contributions.

Build trust.
Leaders demonstrating accountability showcase integrity and commitment to their word. This fosters a culture of trust within the team and organization.

Drive success within the organization.
Accountable leaders contribute to organizational success by ensuring alignment toward common goals. When leaders take responsibility for their actions, they are more likely to establish clear objectives and ensure that everyone is working collaboratively to achieve those goals. This, in turn, leads to improved performance and better outcomes for the organization.

Sometimes, taking accountability for a mistake can be daunting and unsettling. It is hard for people to admit they made a mistake due to the fear of repercussions and the shame of disappointing the people above them. It is not uncommon to witness employees resorting to excuses, placing blame, or even fabricating stories to avoid facing responsibility. It is crucial to recognize that mistakes often present teachable moments and opportunities for learning. Additionally, admitting mistakes openly, discussing them, and moving forward can contribute to personal and professional growth.

A proficient leader fosters an environment where employees feel at ease approaching them, even when they've missed a deadline or made an error. While consequences may exist, creating an open-door policy encourages employees to bring issues to their attention for prompt resolution. It is important to note that employees who witness harsh criticism and punishment that others have received for making mistakes will be more cautious about taking accountability. A leader's accessibility and how they handle such situations play a pivotal role in fostering a transparent and communicative work culture.

Drawing a parallel to parenting, irrespective of whether you have children, everyone can relate to childhood experiences. For instance, addressing a child's tendency to lie requires a candid conversation about the importance of truthfulness, even in challenging situations. Establishing clear consequences for dishonesty while highlighting reduced or no repercussions for honesty encourages openness. This approach, similar to parenting, can be applied in leadership.

Consider this scenario where one of my employees sent out multiple email blasts with errors in the same week due to rushing. On a positive note, she noticed her mistake and came directly to me. I expressed my disappointment, but also my appreciation for her honesty in coming forward and admitting her mistake. I emphasized the need for improvement, the fact that she had to slow down and be careful and suggested practical solutions that included creating a checklist and having another employee proofread before sending. This not only provided guidance but also encouraged a proactive approach to addressing and preventing future errors. The employee's willingness to seek guidance demonstrated the effectiveness of a leadership style that values accountability and growth.

Leaders, like everyone else, are not immune to mistakes. Recalling a personal experience, I once promised my call center manager a new script for a cross-selling promotion by the end of the next day but failed to deliver. When reminded of my oversight, I promptly acknowledged my mistake, apologized, and ensured the task's completion within the hour. This example underscores the importance of accountability and the willingness to admit mistakes, traits essential in effective leadership.

Admitting mistakes is never easy, but it is a crucial aspect of personal and professional growth. If you are intimidated by the prospect of confessing errors to a superior, always remember that leaders are human, too. They understand fallibility and value honesty and accountability just as much as any team member. As my mother always said, "They might be your boss, but they put their pants on the same way you do—one leg at a time." In essence, acknowledging mistakes fosters a culture of trust and growth within any organization.

Chapter 5 - Providing Impactful Guidance and Recognition

"The way to develop the best that is in a person is by appreciation and encouragement."
~Charles Schwab

We have previously discussed role clarity, training, and accountability. All of these are crucial to success, but do not matter if there is no guidance, feedback, and recognition.

Guidance
While it is fantastic that you have invested time and effort into creating manuals and providing initial training for new team members, it is also important to recognize that simply giving them a guide, offering hands-on training, and then setting them free is not the sole recipe for success. Continuous guidance is key.

Guidance for new employees is pivotal for several reasons. It plays a crucial role in their seamless integration into the workplace and significantly contributes to overall organizational effectiveness. It is not just about the initial training; ongoing support and mentorship are essential for sustained success.

importance of Guidance For New Employees Smooth Onboarding Process:
Clear guidance ensures that new employees not only comprehend the company culture, policies, and procedures

but also grasp their practical application in real-world scenarios. While training manuals and documents offer valuable information, they often lack the context and nuanced understanding that personalized guidance provides. New hires benefit from direct interaction with experienced colleagues and managers who can offer insights, answer questions, and provide mentorship tailored to their specific roles and responsibilities.

Smooth onboarding goes beyond simply imparting information; it alleviates stress, fosters a sense of belonging, and cultivates a positive first impression.

Personalized guidance during this crucial period instills confidence in new employees, empowering them to navigate challenges effectively and contribute meaningfully from the outset. By investing in hands-on support and mentorship during the onboarding process, organizations lay the foundation for a successful and fulfilling career trajectory for their newest team members.

Productivity and Job Performance

Guidance on job roles, responsibilities, and expectations helps new employees understand what is expected of them.

Clear expectations help to increase job performance, productivity, and efficiency.

Example - When Sarah joined our marketing team, she diligently studied the training manuals and documents she was provided. However, until she had a one-on-one discussion with her manager about the specific expectations and nuances of her role, she didn't truly understand how to prioritize tasks and collaborate effectively with other departments. This personalized guidance not only clarified her responsibilities but also boosted her confidence and productivity, leading to noticeable improvements in her job performance.

Integrating with the Team

Guidance facilitates introductions to team members and key stakeholders, fostering a sense of belonging.

When employees feel integrated and supported, they adapt quickly and become more valuable team members.

Example - Our new software developer found it challenging to integrate with his team despite reading about their roles and responsibilities in the training manual.

However, after his manager introduced him to each team member individually and scheduled informal meetings to discuss ongoing projects and team dynamics, he quickly felt like a valued part of the team. This guidance not only accelerated his adaptation process but also encouraged collaboration and teamwork.

Understanding Workplace Culture

Guidance on the company values, vision, mission, norms, and communication channels helps new employees adapt to the overall company culture.

Cultural understanding and fit foster a positive work environment and minimize conflict.

Example - A recent hire in our sales department initially struggled to align with our company's culture and communication norms.

Despite reading about our values and mission in the onboarding materials, she found it challenging to apply them in her daily interactions with colleagues and clients.

However, after engaging in one-on-one discussions with her manager about the company's cultural nuances and observing their behavior in various situations, she gained a better understanding of how to embody our values authentically. This personalized guidance not only enhanced her cultural fit but also minimized misunderstandings and conflicts within the team.

Professional Growth:

Guidance on training programs, resources, and career paths allows new employees to plan for their career trajectory and professional development.

Professional growth leads to employee satisfaction, retention, and growth.

Example - A junior accountant aspired to advance his career within our organization but was unsure about the available training programs and career paths.

He explored the resources outlined in company documents but found it overwhelming to navigate them independently. However, after his manager provided personalized guidance on the training opportunities and mapped out potential career trajectories, he felt empowered to create a tailored professional development plan. This guidance not only fueled his enthusiasm for learning but also fostered a sense of direction and purpose in his career journey.

Job Satisfaction

Guidance and support lead to overall job satisfaction. Satisfied employees are more likely to be committed, engaged, and productive.

Example - A customer service representative experienced occasional frustrations in her role despite her dedication to customer satisfaction. Although she appreciated the company's support resources, she needed more personalized guidance to address specific challenges and opportunities for growth.

After her manager scheduled regular coaching sessions to provide constructive feedback and discuss strategies for overcoming obstacles, she felt more valued and supported in her role. This personalized guidance not only boosted her job satisfaction but also increased her motivation to excel and contribute to the team's success.

While crucial to getting new employees up to speed and setting them up for success, guidance continues to be pivotal throughout all employee tenures.

Continual guidance fosters:
Creativity and Innovation

When teams meet regularly with their manager, they not only discuss ongoing projects but also brainstorm new ideas and explore innovative approaches to problem-solving.

This continual guidance empowers team members to think outside the box, resulting in creative solutions that elevate an organization's products and services.

Alignment with Organizational Goals

Through regular check-ins with their manager, employees gain clarity on how their individual contributions align with the company's overarching objectives.

This continual guidance ensures that everyone understands their role in achieving organizational goals and remains focused on shared priorities.

Employee Retention

By providing ongoing support and mentorship, managers demonstrate their commitment to employees' professional growth and success.

This continual guidance fosters a sense of loyalty and investment in the company, reducing turnover rates and retaining top talent.

Team Collaboration

When teams receive regular feedback and guidance from their leaders, they develop stronger bonds and trust among members.

This continual guidance encourages open communication and collaboration, leading to more cohesive and effective teamwork.

Stress and Burnout Reduction

Through regular coaching sessions, managers help employees manage their workloads and prioritize tasks effectively.

This continual guidance prevents burnout by addressing sources of stress and providing support when needed.

Employee Engagement

By actively involving employees in decision-making processes and seeking their input on projects, managers foster a culture of engagement and empowerment.

This continual guidance ensures that employees feel valued and motivated to contribute their best efforts.

Increased Performance, Productivity, and Efficiency

When employees receive ongoing feedback and guidance on their performance, they have the opportunity to course-correct and improve continuously.

This continual guidance leads to higher levels of productivity and efficiency as employees strive for excellence in their work.

Continuous Learning and Development

Through regular training sessions, employees have access to resources and support for their professional development.

This continual guidance encourages lifelong learning and skill enhancement, keeping employees motivated and engaged.

Quicker Adaptation to change

Managers who consistently offer updates and guidance regarding organizational changes facilitate a deeper understanding among employees, enabling them to swiftly adapt. This ongoing support not only reduces resistance to change but also promotes a seamless transition for all stakeholders.

Ongoing support and guidance lead to the sustained success of employees and are also large contributors to a positive organizational culture.

Let's examine a concrete example of proficient guidance in action. During my tenure at a previous company, our team was tasked with booking service appointments, with various departments responsible for different aspects, including the Call Center, Events Team, and Scheduling Team. To ensure cohesion and progress, I implemented weekly collective meetings with the managers from each team.

These meetings served as a platform to discuss progress, address any issues, and brainstorm new ideas and promotions collaboratively.

Following these discussions, we would develop training sessions for all team members to ensure everyone was on board with the new strategies and initiatives.

Moreover, these meetings didn't just end with brainstorming sessions; They also led to the assignment of tasks to each department. Consequently, I would schedule individual weekly meetings with each manager to track progress, address any arising issues, and further explore innovative ideas.

By proactively providing this type of guidance not only did it facilitate the completion of projects, but it also enabled leaders to stay attuned to the pulse of the employees. This approach facilitated swift issue resolution, ensured continuous project momentum, and helped alleviate burnout as leaders maintained a close eye on ongoing developments.

Feedback

For a leader to provide the type of guidance and support needed to set their employees up for success, they must provide ongoing feedback and have regular check-ins and feedback sessions. Regular feedback gives employees insights into their strengths, weaknesses, and areas for improvement.

Unfortunately, many organizations limit feedback to semi-annual and annual reviews, disciplinary actions, or terminations. This practice is inherently unfair and does a disservice to the organization, the team, and the individual employees. No employee should walk into a review feeling surprised or shell-shocked. Ongoing feedback is essential, offering a continuous gauge of performance and areas for growth.

Whether it's a performance review, a write-up, or a termination discussion, employees should be aware of the possibility based on the ongoing feedback they've received.

Transparency in communication ensures that employees are never caught off guard. Conversely, when employees excel, they deserve to be acknowledged, informed, and celebrated during expected positive reviews.

The emphasis on regular feedback not only promotes a culture of openness but also allows for a more informed, engaged, and motivated workforce. It is a proactive approach that aligns employee expectations with organizational goals and fosters a healthier working relationship between leaders and their teams.

Let's examine a scenario from my past experience working for an organization that conducted yearly performance reviews. Unfortunately, apart from these annual evaluations, it was left to the discretion of each department manager whether or not to provide additional feedback on a regular basis. One instance stands out with a regional manager who had been with the company for twenty years. Throughout her tenure, she consistently received positive feedback during her annual reviews and always achieved a 100% bonus. However, during her twenty-first review, she was informed that she had not been meeting her milestones and consequently was terminated.

It came to light that her sales figures were slightly below target at two of the twenty properties under her management. She had been actively working to improve these numbers, but due to the infrequency of feedback sessions with her boss, he was unaware of her efforts and corrective actions. Consequently, the company ended up dismissing a highly tenured employee who had significantly contributed to its success over the years. The repercussions were immediate – four of her loyal employees sought alternative employment, exacerbating the decline in performance at the affected properties and leading to further departures.

This example underscores the importance of ongoing guidance and feedback in the workplace. If the manager had engaged with her sooner upon noticing the declining numbers, the outcome could have been vastly different.

She would have had the opportunity to communicate her awareness of the issue and present her plan to address it. Subsequently, the manager could have established a regular cadence for follow-up discussions to monitor progress and provide support as needed.

Giving effective feedback involves specific approaches and focusing on key areas. Consider the following strategies:

Schedule Regular One-on-One Meetings:

New employees may require more frequent sessions than their tenured counterparts. They benefit from weekly or bi-weekly meetings tailored to their job and experience level, while more tenured employees can have bi-weekly or monthly sessions.

Discuss their feelings, progress, and job satisfaction during these meetings.

Analyze Employee Performance:

- Individual Goals.
- KPIs (Key Performance Indicators).
- Project Outcomes.

Ask Thoughtful Questions:

- What is going well?
- What could be going better?
- Where do you need support?
- What else can I do to help you?

Provide Constructive Feedback and Recognition:

- Celebrate the wins.
- Address areas that could have gone better.
- Provide improvement solutions.

Let's put these approaches into practice:

Kathy is a new employee on a sales team for an organization that sells bathroom renovations. She is provided with two to three appointments per day to visit people's homes, analyze their needs and current bathroom space, and then provide design options and quotes. She has monthly customer closing and revenue goals to hit. She has just finished her training and is embarking on her first week, selling on her own. Jared, Kathy's boss, has set up weekly check-ins every Monday to review the week prior.

Here is how the session goes:

Jared: Hi, Kathy. Congratulations on finishing your first solo week! You did a great job. How do you feel that the week went?

Kathy: I was a little nervous, but overall feel like I am getting the hang of the job and getting more comfortable with my sales pitch every time I go into a prospective customer's home.

Jared: That's great. Ok then, let's look over your numbers. It looks like you missed your numbers by one. While you closed three sales and achieved $30,000 in revenue, we were aiming for four sales and a revenue of $32,000. Nonetheless, this is an impressive start for your first week you should be proud. Since you did miss your numbers by one, do you need some additional support to help you hit one more for next week? Did you have any specific challenges?

Kathy: There were two customers who really seemed interested but needed to think about it, and I am not sure I addressed that objection correctly, as I told them I understood and would follow up in a week.

Jared: Those can be difficult objections to navigate. When customers express hesitation, it's essential to delve deeper into their concerns. You can ask probing questions to understand their reservations better and offer immediate incentives, such as limited-time discounts or financing options, to create urgency. Remember, you can aways call me when you are in the house if you need some support.

Kathy: Thanks, Jared. I will try that this week and let you know how it goes.

Jared: I appreciate your openness in discussing your challenges. Is there anything else you feel you need support or guidance with as you continue in your role?

Kathy: No, that was my only issue. Thanks for the help!

Jared: Remember, each week presents new opportunities for growth and improvement. Don't hesitate to reach out whenever you encounter obstacles or need assistance. Together, we can continue to elevate your performance and achieve success.

This scenario exemplifies Jared's proactive approach to acknowledging Kathy's achievements, setting clear expectations, soliciting her input, and providing valuable support and solutions for performance improvement.

These structured feedback sessions not only provide employees with a platform to express themselves but also allow for a holistic evaluation of their progress, needs, and contributions. Regular feedback, when delivered thoughtfully, contributes to a positive and growth-oriented work environment.

Recognition

"People work for money but go the extra mile for recognition, praise, and rewards."
~Dale Carnegie

While money provides the means to pay bills and enjoy certain freedoms, it doesn't always translate to happiness. I've encountered numerous individuals who, despite having high salaries, find themselves overworked, stressed, and discontented with their jobs. Recognizing your employees is one of the simplest yet most effective ways to foster happiness and encourage hard work. Everyone appreciates positive reinforcement.

Consider the insights from Quantum Workplace Research on the importance of employee recognition (The Importance of Employee Recognition: Statistics and Research (quantum-workplace.com)[4]:

- The third most common reason people leave their jobs is a lack of recognition.
- 52.5% desire more recognition from their immediate supervisors.
- Organizations that employ recognition programs experience 31% lower turnover and 28% lower frustration levels and are 12 times more likely to see positive business outcomes.

It's crucial to acknowledge that recognition can take various forms. Its impact is most significant when employees perceive value in the acknowledgment.

Here are some essential tips for effective recognition:

Recognize Effort and Achievement:
Acknowledge the process and the outcome.

Timeliness Is Key:
Provide recognition promptly, ideally immediately or within a few days of the accomplishment.

Recognition Methods:
Recognition can be expressed through a simple "Thank You," a small gift, a lunch/dinner, or a public acknowledgment. Combining these approaches can also be effective.

---

[4] QuantumWorkplace. (2024). The Importance of Employee Recognition: Statistics and Research: https://www.quantumworkplace.com/future-of-work/importance-of-employee-recognition

Regardless of the method chosen, it's vital to make the recognition personal and sincere. Imagine when you put significant effort into a project, only to receive no feedback.

Contrast that with a scenario where your boss thanked you promptly, acknowledged your hard work, and credited you during a team meeting.

The latter not only boosts morale but also reinforces job satisfaction and a sense of accomplishment. The beauty of the second scenario is that it costs the company nothing yet yields substantial gains by enhancing job satisfaction, reducing turnover, and improving overall productivity and performance.

An experience from one of my roles sheds light on the importance of timely recognition and feedback.

I dedicated significant effort to meticulously crafting an annual promotion calendar, detailing monthly promotional campaigns along with the necessary marketing strategies, budget allocations, and projected outcomes.

I compiled all this information into a comprehensive PowerPoint presentation, complemented by a detailed spreadsheet containing all relevant figures and data. Excited to share my work and eager for feedback, I promptly submitted it to my boss.

However, despite my diligence and the importance of the project, weeks passed without any response. After three weeks of silence, I approached my boss to inquire about her thoughts on the presentation. To my disappointment, she admitted she hadn't even looked at it yet and promised to review it soon. As time went on, a month passed without any feedback or acknowledgment of my efforts. This lack of recognition and delayed feedback was profoundly disheartening. It left me feeling undervalued and demotivated, questioning the significance of investing my time and energy into future projects assigned by my supervisor.

Let's look at a contrasting scenario:

Imagine a marketing team at a tech startup where teamwork and innovation are key to success. Sarah, a marketing associate, has been working tirelessly on a new campaign aimed at launching the company's latest product. As the campaign deadline approaches, Sarah puts in long hours, collaborating with her team members, refining strategies, and ensuring all elements of the campaign are in place.

After the campaign launch, Sarah's efforts yield impressive results. The campaign generates significant buzz, driving a notable increase in website traffic and product inquiries. Recognizing Sarah's dedication and the success of the campaign, her manager, Emily, understood that she needed to quickly recognize Sarah's efforts and achievements.

Emily wastes no time in expressing her appreciation. The following day, she invites Sarah for a brief one-on-one meeting. During the meeting, Emily starts by acknowledging Sarah's hard work and commitment to the project. She highlights specific aspects of Sarah's contribution, such as her creative ideas, attention to detail, and ability to collaborate effectively with team members.

Emily then presents Sarah with a small token of appreciation—a gift card to her favorite coffee shop. Additionally, Emily publicly praises Sarah's efforts during the team's weekly meeting, ensuring that all team members are aware of Sarah's contribution and the impact of her work on the campaign's success.

Sarah feels genuinely valued and recognized for her efforts. The timely recognition not only boosts her morale but also reinforces her commitment to the team and the company's goals. Knowing that her hard work is acknowledged and appreciated motivates Sarah to continue delivering exceptional results in future projects.

In this scenario, Emily effectively applies the essential tips for recognition by acknowledging both the effort and the achievement, providing timely recognition, and using a combination of methods (personal acknowledgment and a small gift). This approach not only strengthens Sarah's engagement and job satisfaction but also fosters a culture of appreciation and recognition within the team.

In addition to rewarding performance, recognizing birthdays and anniversaries and meeting overall company goals are additional avenues to enhance company culture and employee satisfaction. A meaningful way to acknowledge these milestones is through a company-wide announcement accompanied by a small gift or certificate.

For instance, in one company I worked for, all birthdays, anniversaries, and significant accomplishments were highlighted at the monthly company-wide meeting. This created a sense of inclusivity and celebration within the team.

In another organization, employees received a service certificate for each year of their tenure, accompanied by a handwritten note from the CEO. Additionally, a special gift was presented for every five years of service. This personalized approach not only recognized employees for their dedication but also added a personal touch that contributed to a positive and appreciative company culture.

Another great example of recognition was at FOR Energy. As part of each weekly meeting, we could send in recognition for others on our team or in the company. These shout-outs would be read aloud at each meeting and at the company-wide meeting each month.

Numerous companies now offer employee recognition programs facilitated through automated emails and gift options. While these initiatives may lack the personal touch of a note directly from the CEO, they can be enjoyable and motivating.

A case in point is our use of Snappy.com at one of the companies I worked for. Snappy.com allows you to configure automated personalized emails for specific milestones, such as birthdays or work anniversaries. These emails include a personalized note along with a curated selection of enjoyable gifts for the recipient to choose from. While these automated programs add convenience, it is crucial not to overlook the importance of recognizing achievements during company meetings or through personalized expressions of gratitude from leadership, like a card from the executive team.

Incorporating both automated recognition programs and personal gestures ensures a well-rounded approach to acknowledging and appreciating the contributions of employees.

As a leader, I've discovered the profound impact of expressing sincerity and appreciation through gestures like team lunches following significant project successes or milestone achievements.

Additionally, I make it a point to take each team member out to lunch to celebrate their birthdays and provide them with small holiday gifts. In cases where employees work remotely from distant locations and traditional lunch outings aren't feasible, I opt to send them DoorDash or Uber Eats gift cards as a token of appreciation. I also make a point to personally call them to extend birthday wishes or congratulate them on a job well done.

As we strive for continuous improvement, let us not forget that the journey towards exceptional leadership is ongoing. Regularly assess the effectiveness of your guidance, feedback, and recognition programs, seeking feedback from employees to refine and enhance your approach. By embracing these principles, leaders not only set their teams up for success but also contribute to a positive organizational culture where individuals thrive and extraordinary achievements become the norm.

Chapter 6 - Leading, Mentoring, Coaching, and Managing

In the realm of leadership, confusion often arises between wielding authority and fostering true leadership. Many fall into the trap of equating leadership solely with hierarchy, where directives are expected to be followed simply because of one's position. However, effective leadership transcends mere authority, emphasizing mentorship, coaching, and management as essential components.

The Art of Leading: Walking the Talk
Leadership extends beyond rhetoric; it requires actions that align with principles. As a leader, demonstrating your commitment through hard work alongside your team is essential. Being prepared to roll up your sleeves and dive into tasks when necessary is crucial. Leaders who confine themselves to their desks, delegating tasks without involvement, fail to lead successful teams. Employees seek leaders who are supportive, diligent, and unafraid to engage directly when required. Consistent leadership builds trust, nurtures loyalty, and lays the foundation for an exceptional legacy.

As Marketing Director at one of the companies I worked for, I oversaw the events team, a vital department for lead generation. Under my leadership, the team was managed by an Events Manager and supported by part-time Brand Ambassadors, actively participating in 20-40 monthly events. These ranged from sizeable three-day home shows and festivals to small health and wellness fairs. The demanding schedule often placed significant strain on the manager, who occasionally worked seven days a week for extended periods due to short staffing. One afternoon, I noticed the Events Manager looking pale, exhausted, and distant. She had just completed a week filled with at least two events daily during which most Brand Ambassadors were either sick or absent, so she had to work the events.

Normally, her job consisted of taking event attendance, making appointment bookings, Brand Ambassador management, and office responsibilities, including staffing events, managing payments, and completing weekly reports for me. Thus, having to work the events as well added immense pressure. Though I primarily worked from the office, attending meetings and strategizing, I recognized my duty as her leader, especially given my appreciation for her.

I advised her to schedule me for events until the team was fully staffed and encouraged her to take Mondays and Tuesdays off after weekend work for adequate rest and recovery. When she expressed remorse for needing my assistance, I reassured her that apologies were unnecessary. She was immensely grateful and committed to informing me earlier if she felt overwhelmed.

While many leaders ascend through hard work and development, some erroneously believe their role shifts solely to delegation upon reaching leadership positions. This mindset can jeopardize team success. Leaders must be willing to assist their team when necessary rather than stepping in only when too much work forces team members to leave due to lack of support.

When the call center transitioned to reportng under my department, I hired a manager to oversee its operations. A senior employee, who had previously reported to me, expressed reluctance to report to the new manager, citing their hesitation to engage with the team and reliance on delegation. Acknowledging the validity of this concern, I promptly addressed it with the new manager. As a result, within weeks, the manager demonstrated increased inolvement and support.

Leaders foster a culture of mutual support and collaboration by embodying the behaviors and techniques they expect from their teams, ensuring sustained success.

Mentoring with Purpose: Nurturing Growth and Potential

Let us first delve into the distinctions between coaching and mentoring. Although they may intersect in some aspects, they represent distinct and essential approaches. Additionally, it's crucial to note that while guidance and feedback were previously discussed, they serve as integral components in both effective mentoring and coaching.

Coaching:
- Typically conducted one-to-one.
- Emphasizes a formal and structured approach with specific directives and outcomes.
- Focuses primarily on performance enhancement, skill development, and goal attainment.
- Tends to address more immediate issues and initiatives.
- Characterized by its task-oriented and short-term nature.

Mentoring:
- Centers primarily on career development and advancement.
- Entails less structured sessions where mentors guide, advise, and share knowledge. This can be one-on-one or in a group.
- Spans over an extended period to facilitate comprehensive growth.

When examining leading companies worldwide, a significant majority incorporate formal mentoring programs. In fact, according to Guider AI, 84% of all Fortune 500 companies implement formal mentoring programs[5]. Additionally, Mentor Loop reports that companies with mentoring initiatives witnessed profits 18% better than the average. In comparison, those lacking such programs experienced profits 45% worse than the average [6]. Furthermore, Wharton's findings suggest that individuals participating in mentoring programs, whether as mentors or mentees, were promoted 5-6 times more frequently than employees not engaged in such programs[7].

Effective mentoring transcends mere knowledge transfer; it embodies a dedication to guiding others toward their full potential. As a leader, you're not solely there to dictate to your team; yes, you hold authority, but this authoritarian approach undermines both your success and your team's. Instead, aspire to educate and identify teachable moments from successes, errors, challenges, and innovations. Foster an environment that empowers your employees to execute their duties while instilling confidence in the knowledge that you're there for feedback and support. Your team should perceive your commitment to aiding their success and growth.

Consider the following scenario, illustrating the benefits of an effective mentorship program:

In a bustling marketing agency, CEO Sarah is determined to cultivate a culture of growth and development. Recognizing the significance of mentorship, she introduces a program pairing seasoned marketers with junior associates to provide guidance and support.

One such pairing involves Emma, a seasoned marketing strategist, and Alex, a recent graduate eager to kick-start his

---

[5] Mentoring Statistics For 2024 | Guider AI

[6] Mentoring Statistics You Need to Know - 2023, mentorloop.com

[7] Workplace Loyalties Change, but the Value of Mentoring Doesn't," Knowledge at Wharton, upenn.edu

career. Having excelled in her role, Emma understands the value of mentorship and readily accepts the opportunity to mentor Alex.

Their journey begins with a casual coffee chat, during which Emma takes the time to understand Alex's career aspirations. Through their conversation, she learns of Alex's passion for digital marketing and his desire to delve deeper into content creation and social media management.

With this insight, Emma designs a personalized development plan for Alex, outlining specific goals and milestones. She encourages Alex to undertake new projects and offers guidance and feedback along the way.

As Alex navigates his initial assignments, Emma remains a constant source of support and encouragement. When he encounters challenges, Emma shares her experiences and offers practical advice to help him overcome obstacles.

Over time, Alex's confidence grows, and he begins to excel in his role, taking on more responsibility and making meaningful contributions to client projects. Emma is proud to witness Alex's progress and celebrates his achievements with him.

As the mentorship program progresses, Sarah observes a positive shift in the agency's culture. Team members exhibit increased collaboration and support, with junior associates like Alex feeling empowered to take ownership of their work.

By investing in mentorship, Sarah fosters professional growth among her team members and strengthens the agency as a whole. Through the guidance and support of mentors like Emma, junior associates like Alex realize their full potential and thrive in their careers.

In a job market comprising multiple generations and workers with varying expectations, it's imperative to underscore factors that reduce turnover and foster more efficient and content employees.

Dive into mentoring with purpose, exploring how great leaders cultivate environments conducive to growth, resilience, and continuous learning.

Coaching for Success: Building Resilient Teams

No-suck leaders recognize that coaching is more than a nice set of instructions. It is an essential part of a successfully functioning business. Coaching helps employees better understand their tasks, elevate their skills, increase motivation, and highlight any issues in current processes. This leads to a decrease in absenteeism and an increase in productivity.

Let's Look at some numbers obtained from evercoach.com[8]:

"Employees who affirm they've had meaningful discussions with their manager about their goals and strengths in the past half a year are 3.5 times more likely to be engaged."

"The International Coach Federation (ICF) did their homework and found that 70% of people who had coaching reported better work performance, communication skills, and goal achievement."

"Another study by ICF involving various organizations found 86% of those businesses reported that they made their investment in coaching back, primarily due to a boost in productivity."

As you can see, implementing coaching in the workplace can contribute significantly to employee development, performance improvement, and overall organizational success. As highlighted earlier, coaching should be structured and more formal. Thus, having a formalized coaching cadence and an expectation for each session is essential. For example, if you set quarterly goals with your team to ensure you have a pulse on what is getting accomplished and where the team members might need assistance, you might consider having a monthly check-in or coaching session. To make this go smoothly, you will want to address certain things, and having a form filled out by the employee beforehand will ensure they are prepared. The form can be short and address the following items:

---
8 Coaching in the Workplace: Statistics on Employee Performance (evercoach.com)

- List your current goals.
- What is the status of each - Not Started, In Progress, Completed.
- Are you on track to finish each on time? If not, why?
- Where do you need more guidance or assistance?

Let's Put Effective Coaching to Work:

You're a team leader in a marketing agency responsible for managing a team of digital marketers. You've recently implemented a formal coaching cadence to enhance employee development and performance.

1) *Implementation:*
   Setting Expectations:

   At the beginning of each quarter, you set clear goals with your team members. These goals align with the team's objectives and individual professional growth.

   Monthly Check-in Sessions:

   To ensure ongoing support and progress tracking, you schedule monthly coaching sessions with each team member. These sessions provide an opportunity to review goals, address challenges, and provide guidance.

   Preparation:

   Before each coaching session, you ask team members to fill out a coaching form. This form serves as a guide for discussion during the session and ensures that both parties are prepared.

2) *Coaching Form:*
   The coaching form includes the following sections:
   - **Current Goals:** Team members list their current goals for the quarter.

- **Goal Status:** For each goal, team members indicate whether it's Not Started, In Progress, or Completed.
- **Progress Assessment:** Team members assess whether they're on track to finish each goal on time. If not, they identify reasons for delays.
- **Guidance Needed:** Team members specify areas where they require additional guidance or assistance.

3) *Coaching Session:*
During the coaching session, you review the completed form with the team member. You acknowledge their progress, celebrate achievements, and discuss any challenges or barriers they're facing.

Action Plan:

Together, you develop an action plan to address areas needing improvement or additional support. This plan includes specific steps, timelines, and resources to overcome challenges and achieve goals.

Follow-up:

After the coaching session, you follow up with the team members to ensure they're effectively implementing the action plan. You provide ongoing support and encouragement to help them stay on track.

Let's Look at the Benefits:

- ***Structured Approach:*** The formalized coaching cadence provides a structured framework for employee development and goal attainment.
- ***Continuous Improvement:*** Monthly check-in sessions allow for ongoing feedback and course correction, leading to continuous improvement.
- ***Employee Engagement:*** Regular coaching sessions help team members feel supported and valued, leading to increased engagement and motivation.

- **Performance Enhancement:** By addressing challenges and providing guidance, coaching improves performance and overall organizational success.

Leaders who suck are the ones that assign goals and then do not discuss them until they are due. At that point, if the goal is not completed satisfactorily, it is on the leader who did not provide guidance or check-in. Your employees should never be surprised. They should know if they are on track or missing the mark. Is this more work for you? Yes, but it leads to a team performing at their best, motivated to meet their goals, and confident to come to you for support. In the long run, this shows a great leader, and companies thrive under these leaders.

Chapter 7 - Harmonizing Work and Life: Strategies to Avoid Burnout

The landscape of employees, work ethic, and organizational culture has significantly changed in the post-COVID world. Organizations are grappling with whether to bring everyone back to the office or embrace hybrid and remote positions. This shift has led employees to seek more flexibility in their work, making them discerning about job choices and contributing to staff shortages in many companies.

I once worked for a manager who believed in a constant work pace, requiring the team to be available around the clock. Calls at night, early mornings, and even during vacations were the norm. I vividly remember a week when I worked nine consecutive days in two different time zones. When I requested a day off, my manager acknowledged it but emphasized that I was a salaried employee expected to work as many days as needed.

Despite understanding her perspective, I prioritized my well-being and time with my family and took the day off. I also knew that not taking the day off meant that I would not be working at my full potential because I was so tired. Returning to work refreshed, I felt ready to devote myself entirely to the job. Fortunately, there were no repercussions for my decision, although my manager seemed less surprised when I subsequently requested time off after enduring prolonged work stretches. Her insistence on round-the-clock availability ultimately fostered a culture of high turnover and discontent among employees.

Another example of detrimental leadership is that many companies applaud employees who work while sick or pull all-nighters. Working while sick compromises performance and risks spreading illness to colleagues. Similarly, employees who work all day and late into the night will likely experience reduced efficiency the following day.

Leaders must recognize that overworking employees to the point of burnout diminishes productivity and leaves employees stressed. David Ballard of the American Psychological Association describes burnout as exhaustion, difficulty concentrating, health issues, constant preoccupation with work, frustration, decreased job satisfaction, personal problems at work and home, negative attitude, and neglect of self-care[9].

Extraordinary leaders prioritize a work-life balance to prevent employee burnout, leading by example. While recognizing the occasional need for extended hours due to deadlines or events, leaders should also value time off for self-care and family. Additionally, leaders should pay attention to their team members, identify signs of stress or burnout, and offer support.

I once noticed a member of my team growing increasingly frustrated, and I was uncertain about the cause. Sensing his distress, I took him aside to inquire about the situation. He confided in me, revealing that he had been working late into the evenings and rising early to complete his workload. He admitted feeling exhausted and expressed concern about his strained relationship with his girlfriend due to their lack of quality time together.

I assured him he should always feel comfortable approaching me in such circumstances. I emphasized that there's no reason he should be expected to consistently work outside regular hours. If he found it challenging to manage his workload within the confines of the workday, I offered

---

9 10 Signs You're Burning Out -- And What To Do About It (forbes.com

to assist him in reviewing his tasks and adjusting priorities or relieving him of specific responsibilities if necessary.

Initially hesitant, he expressed reluctance, viewing seeking help from his boss as a sign of weakness. I promptly countered this notion, explaining that it demonstrated proactive behavior and a commitment to personal well-being and professional responsibilities. I also emphasized the detrimental effects of burnout on productivity and the importance of addressing challenges before they escalate.

After our discussion, he agreed to reassess his workload, and together we reprioritized his tasks. From that point forward, he felt more comfortable approaching me whenever he encountered difficulties.

I had the privilege of working under an exceptional CMO and visionary. Despite having four children and enduring a daily commute of an hour and a half each way into the city for work, she skillfully maintained a balance that allowed her to be present for family dinners, take vacations, and attend her kids' school activities and sporting events.

During a lunch and learn session, one of the corporate accounting employees asked about her ability to excel as a CMO and a mother. Her insightful response was that she could be effective in both roles but not simultaneously. She explained her strategy: when at work, she devoted herself entirely to her professional responsibilities, and when at home, she was fully committed to being with her family. She refrained from answering work calls unless there was an emergency during family time, and she avoided working at home until her kids were asleep, and only if absolutely necessary. This deliberate compartmentalization allowed her to excel in her career while ensuring meaningful and focused time with her family.

Recognizing the importance of downtime, especially earned paid time off, is crucial for sustaining high productivity, job satisfaction, and employee loyalty.

Leaders must resist giving positive reinforcement for employees who work when they're sick. It must be understood that sick employees need rest to recover and perform at their best. Setting clear expectations about burnout, time off, and sick leave fosters a healthy work environment where employees feel comfortable approaching their leaders.

While there may be instances of employees attempting to take advantage, clear communication of roles, goals, and expectations, coupled with accountability, ensures that everyone contributes to the team's success. When employees express stress, leaders can assist by understanding their workload, helping with prioritization, and addressing any time management issues. A proactive and empathetic leadership approach prevents burnout and fosters a positive work environment.

Example - What do you do when your employee comes into work very sick?

At a bustling tech startup, the CEO, Adam, has always emphasized the importance of maintaining a healthy work-life balance. He firmly believes that downtime, including earned paid time off (PTO), is crucial for sustaining high productivity, job satisfaction, and employee loyalty.

One day, Adam notices Sarah, one of his team's top performers, coughing and looking visibly unwell at her desk. Concerned, Adam approaches Sarah to inquire about her well-being. Sarah, eager to meet deadlines and not wanting to let her team down, brushes off her symptoms, insisting that she's fine and can continue working.

Adam listens attentively but gently reminds Sarah of the company's policy regarding sick leave. He explains that while dedication to work is admirable, it's equally important to prioritize one's health. Adam assures Sarah that taking a sick day when necessary is acceptable and even encouraged, to ensure she can recover fully and perform at her best upon return.

Sarah initially hesitates, expressing concern about falling behind on her tasks. However, Adam reassures her that the team will support her and that her health takes precedence.

He offers to help redistribute her workload or adjust deadlines to alleviate stress.

Grateful for Adam's understanding and support, Sarah agrees to take the day off to rest and recover. True to his word, Adam ensures that Sarah's absence doesn't disrupt project timelines, demonstrating his commitment to maintaining a healthy work environment.

As a result of Adam's proactive approach to sick leave and prioritizing employee well-being, Sarah returns to work feeling refreshed and grateful for the company's supportive culture. She continues to be a dedicated and productive team member, knowing that her health is valued and respected by leadership.

Time Management

Effective time management and organizational skills are qualities that some individuals possess naturally, while others acquire them through learning and practice. However, many people need help with these skills and may face burnout due to their inefficiencies. As a leader, it is crucial to embody efficiency and strong time management in order to assist employees who grapple with these challenges.

I once supervised an Events Manager who, despite her intelligence and creativity, struggled with disorganization. This resulted in forgetfulness and a growing backlog of tasks, leaving her feeling constantly overworked. Her responsibilities included researching, booking, paying for, and staffing events. Additionally, she managed a team of Brand Ambassadors, ensuring they had event supplies and handled hiring, firing, training, motivating, and holding them accountable to their goals.

Recognizing the need for intervention, I sat down with her one day and shared my approach to structuring my day, prioritizing projects, and handling unforeseen challenges. She welcomed the guidance and promptly began implementing the tips I provided. Some individuals simply need advice on organizing themselves, while other's lack of organization and time management may be a larger issue that makes them more suitable for another role with more structure.

Here is my daily structure for a typical work day:

1. Reviewing my calendar to note meetings and deadlines.
2. Checking my To-Do list to ensure I'm on track with all tasks.
3. Using a notebook or planner to maintain a running log, date each page, and mark completed projects with a check mark.
4. Reading new and starred emails, and responding promptly to those that can be quickly addressed.
5. Assessing tasks from emails, adding them to my to-do list, and informing the sender that I've received their email and am working on their request.
6. Listening to voicemail messages and proceeding with the same process as step 5.
7. Working through my task list, starting with quick tasks and moving on to time-sensitive priorities.
8. At the end of the day, reviewing my accomplishments and creating a list for the next day to carry over any unfinished tasks.

One of the most valuable pieces of advice I offered to the Events Manager and other employees is to use a calendar. In today's digital age, nearly everyone has a calendar on their phone and email. Incorporating your projects into the calendar and allowing ample time for completion before deadlines is essential.

Planning to finish projects 24 to 48 hours ahead of schedule allows for review and any necessary revisions. If the scheduled tasks still need to be completed, move them to the next day. Calendar reminders should be set to alert you when it's time to work on each project. This proactive approach helps manage your workload and facilitates incorporating unexpected meetings or projects that may arise during the day, providing a structured and adaptable schedule.

Numerous employees often need help with the challenge of being entangled in a continuous cycle of meetings, leaving minimal time for actual work. A practical approach to mitigate this issue is to implement time blocks. Schedule dedicated time blocks daily for essential tasks, lunch, and other priorities. Take a look at the calendar example below; it shows scheduled meetings, tasks that need to be completed, as well as blocks for reviews, emails, calls, and to-do's:

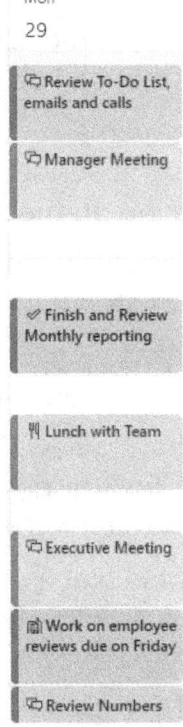

Remember, you cannot pour from an empty cup. Failing to be mindful of your and your employees' time may result in burned-out and dissatisfied team members who struggle to maintain productivity. Every individual requires moments for rest and self-care. Deprived of these essential elements, individuals cannot perform effectively as employees, parents, friends, or even for their own well-being.

Chapter 8 - A Guide to Self-Care and Continuous Personal Growth

As leaders, our journey is dynamic and demanding, filled with the responsibility of guiding others towards success. Amidst the many tasks and challenges, we overlook a crucial element — ourselves. This chapter will explore strategies that nurture your well-being and help you lead with resilience and authenticity.

Leadership comes with challenges and pressures, but taking care of oneself is pivotal to success. It is very easy to get caught up in our work and personal lives to the extent that we do not make time for ourselves. However, it is essential to realize that you cannot pour from an empty cup, meaning you are not good to your family, friends, team, or yourself if you are constantly stressed and burnt out. This means that you need to make time to nurture yourself and fill your cup back up. If you think you are too busy and there is no way to make this happen, change your mindset to "If I make time to nurture myself, I will be a better _____ (fill in the blank- Parent, Employee, Leader, Teacher)."

How do you carve out time for yourself when you have a busy schedule?
Wake up earlier:

Waking up earlier might initially sound daunting, and I completely empathize — it did to me, too. However, my outlook underwent a profound transformation after delving into a book on crafting a morning routine that fosters health, happiness, and success. This book served as a catalyst, encouraging me to deliberately allocate time for movement, reading, meditation, journaling, and visualization each morning.

The insights in this book provided practical tips on time allocation for these activities and how to be fully present and engaged during this sacred morning time. I recommend adopting a healthy morning routine for those lacking one.

Previously, my belief centered around squeezing in every last minute of sleep, rushing through the morning routine to get myself and my child ready for the day, and hustling into the office with no room for deviation. The result? I had stress, impatience, and an edgy disposition when I reached work.

However, incorporating the practices outlined in this book changed the game. Suddenly, my mornings ceased to feel rushed, and upon arriving at work, I found myself in a positive mindset, ready to tackle any challenges thrown my way. This shift enhanced my well-being and positively impacted my effectiveness and resilience throughout the day.

Here's a glimpse of my routine:
- I wake up at 5:15 am.
- Start the day with a refreshing glass of water (which I prepare the night before and keep by my bedside).
- Brush my teeth; this simple act helps awaken my senses.
- Dedicate three minutes to reciting my affirmations (I have four affirmations that I close my eyes and repeat aloud three times each).
- Spend another three minutes journaling.
- Engage in a thirty-minute workout session. I preselect a workout the night before using my Bodi app or opt for a treadmill walk or bike ride.
- Listen to a five-minute meditation.

- o I choose a meditation from YouTube or the Calm App based on what resonates with me that morning.
- Following this roughly forty-five-minute routine, I prepare for the day ahead.

Given my early wake-up time, ensuring adequate sleep is crucial, so I aim to be in bed between 9 pm and 10 pm. Even on nights when sleep eludes me or I retire later, I remain committed to rising early. Consistency is paramount, and adhering to this routine—even when fatigued—significantly enhances my daily experience. During weekends, I allow myself to indulge in a bit of extra rest, rising at 7:30 am to commence my routine.

Schedule Daily Self-Care On Your Calendar

We all use some kind of planner, whether it is our calendar on our phone, our work calendar, or a paper planner. Work Meetings and life responsibilities account for the majority of our day. To ensure you have time for yourself, schedule 30-60 minutes of daily self-care time on your calendar. This can be in the morning, on a lunch break, before bed, or whatever works best for you. This time is your time to do what nurtures your soul. Some ideas for this time include - taking a walk, hiking, napping, meditating, or journaling.

Swap Mindless Phone Scrolling and Television Viewing for Self-Care

Human beings spend an excessive amount of time on their electronics. It is so important to take a break and disconnect for a little bit. Your electronics are not nurturing your soul or filling your cup. Take 30-60 minutes to disconnect and prioritize yourself over your electronics.

How to Practice Self-Care

We have established the importance of self-care and how to fit it into your schedule. Let's discuss some good ways that leaders can prioritize self-care while guiding others:

Set Boundaries - Establish clear boundaries between work and personal life. This means ensuring time for family and personal interests to mitigate burnout.

Here are some great ways to set boundaries:

- Let your team know that after a particular time, you are with your family or at an activity and will not answer emails, calls, and texts from work unless there is an emergency.
- Commit to being home for dinner with your family.
- Make family/friend time technology-free.
- Respect your team's boundaries; if you do not call them late at night or early in the morning during their off time, they will realize this is a critical expectation and respect your boundaries.

Practice Mindfulness. This can be done through meditation or just sitting in silence. It can also be done in nature while walking or hiking alone and just being with yourself and your thoughts. These practices will help you gain perspective, open your mind, and reduce stress.

Mindfulness activities you can engage in include:

- Take an hourly break from your computer for 5-10 minutes to walk and rest your eyes.
- Wake up and sit in silence for 5-10 minutes.
- When feeling stressed, practice closing your eyes and inhaling for a count of 7, holding for a count of 4, and exhaling for a count of 7. Do this at least three times.
- Meditate.
    - You can find multiple free meditations on YouTube.
    - You can download a meditation app.
    - I use either the Calm app or YouTube.
- Journal.

- Freewrite: Spend some time jotting down whatever comes to your mind. You may find that you need to write about a problem that has been causing you stress, a decision you are trying to make, or even your upcoming priorities.
- Create a gratitude journal and write about what you are grateful for daily. Incorporate that healthy morning routine.

Delegate Effectively. Have you ever heard that the only way to get things done correctly is to do them yourself? This needs to be revised; it is the opposite of helping your team advance and having time for yourself. Thus, make sure you are allowing your team to do their jobs and delegating what should be their responsibilities and not yours.

Let's examine a real-life scenario to illustrate the impact of ineffective delegation. During one of my previous roles, I worked under a manager who adamantly refused to delegate any tasks related to managing the marketing budget. This included even the most mundane responsibility of inputting invoice amounts onto a spreadsheet.

Consequently, every month, as the deadline for the budget review with the Executive team loomed, my manager would find herself spending countless hours scrambling to locate invoices and meticulously inputting data into her spreadsheet. This arduous process left her with minimal time to focus on her essential duties and responsibilities.

Moreover, the mounting pressure of impending deadlines resulted in her working tirelessly around the clock during the week leading up to each meeting. This relentless cycle not only took a toll on her well-being but also caused her to neglect her team and family.

By refusing to delegate tasks effectively, my manager inadvertently deprived herself of valuable time and energy that could have been allocated toward more strategic endeavors. This ultimately led to increased stress, burnout, and a significant imbalance between work and personal life.

If she had delegated the task of inputting the numbers into the spreadsheet to someone on the team, she would have only needed to review the completed sheet and prepare her presentation. This simple adjustment could have saved her significant time and alleviated the stress it was causing her every month.

Continuous Learning. There is always something new to learn. Invest time in personal and professional development. Attend workshops, read, listen to podcasts, and stay updated on industry trends.

A fantastic method for crafting a successful strategy to achieve your goals of continuous improvement and growth is to develop a personalized learning plan. This plan serves as a comprehensive guide, encompassing your goals, action items, timelines, metrics, and progress reflections to keep you focused and on the path to success. It goes beyond being a mere checklist; it becomes a personal commitment—a contract with yourself, affirming your desire to complete these tasks and recognizing the paramount importance of continuous improvement. Take a moment to reflect on what you envision for your plan. Then, refer to Appendix A and complete the Personalized Learning Plan Template to initiate this transformative journey.

Regular Exercise. Regular exercise is vital for your physical and mental well-being. Integrate consistent physical activity into your routine to enhance energy levels and alleviate stress. It is essential to recognize that there are various ways to incorporate self-care, including exercise, into your schedule. You do not need to dedicate hours at a gym to experience the benefits of exercise.

As a working mom, I have discovered that one of the most convenient ways to include movement into my day is by utilizing resources like YouTube or fitness apps such as Bodi, allowing me to work out in the comfort of my home. This flexibility enables me to choose workouts that align with my schedule. On some days, I may have an hour, while on others,

I might have only 25 minutes. When a home workout is not feasible, I prioritize taking breaks during my workday to walk for 20-30 minutes. Even if I split the time into ten-minute increments, ensuring I get it done is a non-negotiable part of my routine.

Healthy Lifestyle and the Benefits of a Good Night's Rest

Pay attention to your diet, sleep patterns, and overall health. A balanced lifestyle supports sustained energy and resilience in facing challenges. How many hours per night are you sleeping? Research shows that most adults benefit from 7-9 hours of sleep. Sleeping less than 6 hours can lead to many issues, including making the body more susceptible to disease[10].

According to verywellhealth.com, a full night's sleep regulates blood sugar, decreases stress levels, decreases inflammation, helps with weight loss and maintenance, improves coordination and balance, increases energy, keeps your memory sharp, repairs cells and tissues, increases school and work productivity and helps keep your heart and blood vessels healthy. Like the rest of your self-care routine, sometimes you need to have a plan to make sure this happens.

Tips to ensure a full night's sleep:

- Go to bed at the same time every night. This ensures your body gets into a healthy sleep routine.
- Turn off all electronics at least an hour before going to sleep. Technology's light stimulates your system and promotes alertness.
- Drink a cup of Chamomile tea. Chamomile tea helps to calm the system.
- Do some deep breathing or meditation before bed.
    - There are relaxation apps. One is called Calm, which has guided sleep meditations and stories.

---

10 10 Health Benefits of Sleep (verywellhealth.com)

- o YouTube offers free meditation videos to help you fall asleep.

  *You can do these right before you go to sleep, as you will just be listening to the meditation and not looking at the light coming from the phone.

- Practice some nightly relaxation yoga poses.

  - o Visit <u>Yoga for Sleep: 15 Poses to Help You Get Better Rest (yogajournal.com)</u> to learn 15 poses that help to promote sleep.

While sleep is crucial for self-care and health, so is good nutrition. Unfortunately, many individuals choose processed and unhealthy food for convenience. In our busy lives, the idea of food preparation can be overwhelming, coupled with the misconception that eating healthy is prohibitively expensive. However, the long-term costs of health issues such as clogged arteries, heart problems, and diabetes far outweigh the initial savings from opting for quick, cheap meals like 99-cent tacos from Jack-in-the-Box. In addition, unhealthy foods laden with grease and sugar zap your energy, make you feel ill, and decrease your overall productivity. Many people undervalue the impact of food on our productivity. Think about a car. You feed a car gas, and it reliably gets you to and from the places you need to be. If you feed it corn syrup, it will break down. Your body is no different. If you fuel it with unhealthy foods, you will feel sluggish, have trouble concentrating, and hit that afternoon slump. You need fuel to perform like a car needs fuel to run.

Let's tackle how to make nutritious choices and simplify meal preparation to save time. Cooking at home is usually much healthier than dining out. For those who don't enjoy cooking or seek convenience, subscribing to a food service can be a viable option. Services like Hello Fresh, Home Chef, Sun Basket, and Blue Apron offer nutrient-dense foods, providing pre-cooked meals or kits with recipes for DIY preparation.

Many of these services cater to dietary preferences such as low-carb, paleo, or vegan.

I've found that planning reduces the likelihood of dining out. A lack of planning often leads to takeout for the sake of convenience. To streamline the process, I dedicate time over the weekend to browse Pinterest, Instagram, and AllRecipes for meal ideas. I select weekly recipes and allocate 2-3 hours on Sundays to prepare meals. I aim for balanced meals incorporating protein, carbohydrates, and vegetables. Casseroles, in particular, are convenient to make and store for later consumption. If leftovers aren't your preference, consider preparing meals and freezing them for future use. Also important are the snack choices we make throughout the day. The benefits of choosing a healthy snack like almonds, yogurt, cheese, fruit, or veggies far outweigh candy, cookies, and chips. Healthy snacks will keep your motor running throughout the day.

Build a Strong Support System

Cultivate a network of peers, mentors, or friends who understand the challenges of leadership. Share experiences, seek advice, and offer support to one another. Everyone needs someone to vent to and share knowledge. Other leaders are the most beneficial to do this with for work issues. In the same way, having a robust personal support system is also essential. If you are a busy parent with challenges, other parents are the best people to talk to.

If you don't have an established network, there are numerous effective ways to build one. Consider attending various networking events in your local area; you can find these events by searching online or checking platforms like meetup.com for activities that align with your interests. Additionally, joining social media groups can be an excellent strategy. I'm a member of several online groups related to parenting, nutrition/lifestyle, food preparation, and business on platforms like Facebook, LinkedIn, and Instagram. Engaging in these communities can provide valuable opportunities to connect with like-minded individuals and expand your network.

Vacation and Downtime

This aspect is crucial yet often overlooked, as many individuals neglect the importance of taking time off. It's common to hear people mention how they've used up all their vacation days due to previous absences or sick leave. Consequently, they find themselves unable to take a proper vacation. Everyone needs to have scheduled breaks and holidays to recharge mentally and physically. Disconnecting from work-related communication during these periods is vital to fully enjoy the benefits of relaxation and ensure a genuine break from professional responsibilities.

Vacations don't necessarily have to be extravagant, weeks-long getaways. Even a few days off at home can provide significant rejuvenation. Remember, you've earned this vacation time, and utilizing it is for your benefit and contributes positively to your family, company, and team. Taking the time to recharge ultimately enhances your productivity, creativity, and overall well-being, making it a valuable investment in your personal and professional life. So, make sure to prioritize and utilize your vacation time wisely.

Cultivate Hobbies

Pursuing hobbies and activities outside of work is crucial to maintaining a healthy work-life balance. Engaging in activities that bring joy and fulfillment provides a welcome break from professional responsibilities and contributes to a well-rounded and contented life.

Consider exploring various hobbies, such as hiking, painting, gardening, playing a musical instrument, or participating in a sports league. Dedicating time to these pursuits allows you to recharge creatively, reduce stress, and foster personal growth. Moreover, sharing your hobbies with others can lead to meaningful connections and a sense of community.

Remember that cultivating hobbies isn't just a leisure activity; it's an investment in your overall well-being. It provides an avenue for self-expression, relaxation, and the development of new skills. So, as you navigate work demands, carve out time for activities that bring you genuine satisfaction and contribute to the holistic balance of your life.

Remember, effective leadership starts with a leader who is in good physical and mental condition. By prioritizing self-care benefits, the leader sets a positive example for the team, fostering a healthier and more productive work environment.

Chapter 9 - Things that Make You Go, Hmmm...

I am the leader I am today largely due to the leaders I have worked under. Each has taught me valuable lessons, shaping my ability to guide others effectively. This is also why I have the knowledge and experience to write this book.

Take a second to ponder these far too often utilized quotes:

> "It's not my problem; figure it out on your own."
> "You're lucky to have a job here."
> "Win at all costs."

These quotes personify lousy leadership. None of them lead to favorable results, provide support, or ensure employees are successful. Think about what you say to your employees and ensure it is not one of the lines quoted above.

I wrote this chapter to reflect on some of the challenging experiences my friends, colleagues, and I have faced. I hope these anecdotes offer readers valuable lessons and perhaps a few lighthearted moments.

I was once in a meeting with a leader who asked me what letting go of two key employees, both managers, would free me up to do. I thought my answer was obvious – "their jobs". However, he responded by saying that I did not answer the question. I told him I was confused, and he was not able to elaborate enough to allow me to change my answer.

My friend was up for a promotion promised to her for months. However, when the promotion time arrived, her boss informed her that she could only get it if she took on the additional responsibilities associated with the promotion for an entire year. Only after completing the year would she receive the title promotion and raise. She immediately started looking for another job and made a plan to leave by the end of the year, which she did.

I worked for a company that brought in a consultant. During a meeting, the consultant informed all the managers that they needed to complete a project to help him decide if they were suitable for their roles. He explicitly stated that they would lose their jobs if the results indicated they were not the right fit. Essentially, he asked them to put in work that could cost them their job.

While conducting annual corporate reviews, a manager asked one of my friends to sign off on a document falsely stating that certain services were performed. Authentic leadership involves maintaining integrity and avoiding putting employees in risky and questionable positions.

While at one of my jobs, our marketing budget was slightly overspent for one month. Instead of truthfully presenting it to the CEO, the CMO asked me to manipulate the budget to make it appear as if everything was in line. This is unethical, and there is a paper trail, and this lie will be uncovered.

A friend of mine worked on an assigned project for months. When he was finished, his boss took it and presented it as his own to his leadership, who loved it. My friend never received any credit for it. There are numerous instances where leaders take their team members' ideas and hard work and present them as their own. I have personally experienced this, as have many of my friends and former colleagues. Leaders who lack integrity and fail to support their teams hinder growth and loyalty. Such actions harm the individuals involved and negatively impact morale, leading to decreased productivity as people become hesitant to share ideas.

My friend and I were employed by a company led by individuals deeply rooted in their religion. Representatives from their church were regularly dispatched to employees' homes to convert them. Furthermore, it was not uncommon to overhear members of the leadership team questioning female employees about their marital status and suggesting they should be at home caring for their children instead of working. This created tension and awkwardness in the office and led to high turnover, including both of us, who ended up leaving after a very short stint there. Beyond being ethically questionable, such behavior can potentially result in lawsuits.

My first job in high school was at a restaurant owned by my next-door neighbors. Initially, I occasionally babysat for them until I took the restaurant job. One day, one of the owners expressed dissatisfaction with my performance and suggested that I could keep my job only if I babysat for her every Saturday. This proposition led me to quit my job at their restaurant and put an end to babysitting altogether. Such situations highlight the importance of fair and respectful treatment in the workplace.

I was employed by a small family-owned company and reported directly to the owner. During meetings in the boardroom, he would burp, fart, abruptly walk out and not return, and openly discuss his digestive issues like diarrhea. Additionally, he was known for frequently yelling and using profanity when addressing employees. Such conduct was unprofessional and created an uncomfortable and unproductive work environment.

A colleague of mine dedicated three years to helping her adopted dog overcome skin, muscle, and aggression problems, but his condition continued to worsen. The dog began attacking her and her other dog, prompting the vet to advise euthanasia due to the severity of the issues. The decision to put her beloved pet down was one of the toughest things she had ever faced. Seeking support, she informed her boss about the situation and took a day off. Surprisingly, her boss' response lacked empathy; there was no expression of sympathy as he told her it was fine to take one day off, but he absolutely wanted her back in the office the next day. Upon her return, there was no inquiry into her well-being. He never even addressed what she had been through. The incident had little impact on her boss, as all he recognized was the loss of productivity rather than the suffering she was experiencing. This lack of understanding left her feeling unsupported during a difficult time. She is still with the company but not as engaged or passionate about her work.

As we reflect on these challenging experiences, we are reminded that leadership is a complex journey filled with moments that test our character, resilience, and ability to navigate difficult situations. Each story in this chapter underscores the importance of ethical leadership, empathy, and the impact leaders can have on their team members.

In the face of adversity, the true measure of a leader lies not just in their ability to achieve results but in their commitment to maintaining integrity, treating others with respect, and fostering a supportive work environment. The anecdotes presented here highlight instances where leadership fell short, actions were ethically questionable, and empathy was notably absent.

As leaders, we must recognize our profound impact on the lives of those we lead. Whether navigating personnel changes, honoring promises, or upholding ethical standards, every decision shapes our teams' culture and our organizations' success.

In sharing these stories, I intend not to criticize but to shed light on the diverse challenges leaders and their teams face. I hope readers find resonance in these narratives, drawing valuable lessons that inspire growth, compassion, and a commitment to fostering positive workplace cultures.

There is no one-size-fits-all approach to leadership or dealing with any of the situations mentioned above. However, there are always right and wrong ways to handle things if you aim to keep a motivated and productive staff. Throughout my career, I've learned the importance of showing respect to all employees and being willing to listen and offer support. Actively listening, without distractions, helps leaders understand what their team and company need from them. For example, during meetings with employees, it's crucial to close your computer and refrain from looking at your phone to give them your undivided attention. This not only demonstrates good behavior for the employee but also illustrates your commitment to helping them succeed.

Good leaders should be firm when needed but also understand that mistakes are human and will be made. Even great leaders make mistakes. It's crucial to view mistakes as learning opportunities. Reflecting on the example where an employee sent out multiple email blasts with mistakes, I could have chosen to react with anger or write her up. Instead, we had a firm conversation about the seriousness of the mistakes and worked together to find ways she could avoid making them in the future. This approach offered solutions rather than just a punishment session.

It's important to consider how you have wanted to be treated by your supervisors and avoid emulating toxic behavior that may have influenced your decision to change jobs or workplaces.

Ultimately, the lessons learned from both great and terrible leaders have shaped me into the leader I am today. The insights gained from these experiences have shaped my leadership legacy and fueled my desire to contribute to the leadership discourse and guide those navigating their leadership journeys.

Chapter 10 - Leaving Your Leadership Legacy

"The greatest leader is not necessarily the one who does the greatest things. He is the one that gets the people to do the greatest things."

~ Ronald Reagan

Think about this - What will you be remembered for?

As a leader and a mom, I want to leave my mark on my child and my employees by instilling values that include ethics, fairness, sincerity, kindness, listening, and social-emotional intelligence. It is important to me to do things that matter, like helping my son grow up happy and successful and helping my employees cultivate careers they love and can advance in. Success is so much more than just making a lot of money; it is having job/career satisfaction, working to make a difference and leave my mark, and making enough money to keep my family safe and materially comfortable. I want to ensure that I am not just living my life and working to work but making a difference for myself and the people in my life.

A leadership legacy refers to a leader's lasting impact and imprint on individuals, organizations, and the broader community long after their leadership role has ended. It encompasses the positive and enduring contributions, values, and influences that shape an organization's culture, performance, and direction. A leadership legacy is not only about achievements or results; it also involves cultivating a positive and sustainable leadership culture. This can include fostering a sense of empowerment, encouraging innovation, promoting ethical behavior, and developing the next generation of leaders. A leadership legacy is the mark a leader makes on the people they lead.

Your leadership and life legacies are personal to you. As you think about what you want those to be. Here are some key elements that may help you to shape your legacy:

1. Impact on Others.
2. Community and Social Impact.
3. Innovation and Adaptability.
4. Organizational Culture.
5. Impact on People.
6. Values and Principles.

Think about the people you look up to and turn to for advice and mentorship. Why do you choose them? What mark have they left on you?

Reflecting on those I admire and seek guidance from, I consider individuals whose influence has left a lasting mark on my perspective and actions. One such person is Stephen Covey, renowned for his work on the "Seven Habits of Highly Effective People." Amidst the plethora of books I encountered during college, Covey's work stood out and has since become a foundational framework for my approach to success. His seven habits truly indicate success and should be implemented by anyone, whether running their own business or working for someone else.

Additionally, my father has played a pivotal role as my business mentor. As an entrepreneur with a track record of owning several successful ventures, he has imparted invaluable lessons. My dad has taught me the value of finding solutions to problems rather than reacting emotionally. Like Covey, my dad has always emphasized the importance of proactivity over reactivity. He has also demonstrated the significance of cultivating relationships and networking. With a vast network, many people seek his advice, invite him to sit on boards, and request his presentations. His ability to build rapport and forge lasting relationships is one of the keys to his success. I always appreciate hearing his work colleagues and customers express their admiration for working with him.

Through his guidance, I've come to appreciate the significance of hard work, self-sufficiency, and the profound impact one can make in the business world. His example has shaped my understanding of success, emphasizing the importance of leaving a positive and influential legacy that others can admire when striving for success.

These are just two examples of people who have left their mark on me as a leader and have helped me to shape the type of leader I strive to be and the legacy I want to leave.

As I think about the legacy I want to leave as a leader, it includes:

- *Inspiration and vision that motivates:* Inspiring others through a compelling vision and passion for achieving common goals.

- *Empowerment to utilize skills and experience to make a difference:* Providing individuals with the autonomy and support to leverage their talents and expertise effectively.

- *Investment in development:* Committing resources and effort to foster continuous growth and learning among team members.

- *Ethical Leadership:* Upholding integrity, honesty, and fairness in all decisions and actions, setting a high standard for moral conduct.

- *A culture of innovation:* Cultivating an environment where creativity, experimentation, and risk-taking are encouraged to drive innovation and progress.

- *A backbone for adaptability:* Building resilience and flexibility within the organization to navigate challenges and seize opportunities in a rapidly changing environment.

- *Strong communication skills:* Communicating effectively and transparently, fostering open dialogue, and ensuring clarity in conveying goals and expectations.
- *A track record of results and achievements:* Demonstrating a history of delivering tangible outcomes and making meaningful contributions to each organization's success.

As I think about the legacy I want to leave as a mom, it is not so dissimilar to my leadership legacy, and it includes:

- *Strong values and ethics:* Instilling in my son a deep sense of integrity, honesty, and compassion, serving as a moral compass in his life.
- *Love for learning:* Nurturing curiosity and thirst for knowledge, encouraging my son to explore, discover, and embrace lifelong learning.
- *Strong work ethic and ambition:* Modeling diligence, perseverance, and a drive for excellence, inspiring my son to pursue his passions with determination and dedication.
- *Resilience and coping skills:* Equipping my son with the resilience and coping mechanisms to navigate life's challenges with grace and fortitude, fostering his emotional well-being.
- *Passion and purpose:* Encouraging my son to pursue his interests and dreams with enthusiasm and purpose, empowering him to lead a fulfilling life aligned with their values.
- *Health and well-being:* Prioritizing physical, mental, and emotional health, teaching my son the importance of self-care and balance in maintaining overall well-being.

- *Lasting memories:* Creating cherished moments and experiences that strengthen family bonds and leave a lasting imprint of love, joy, and connection.
- *Financial stability:* Providing a stable and secure foundation for my son's future, imparting financial literacy and responsibility to ensure his economic well-being.

I hope that one day, if someone asks him whom he looks up to, I will be one of the people he mentions!

Taking time to shape your life legacies is like creating a roadmap for your life. It is the compass by which you will make personal and work decisions, set goals, and live your life. Make this an activity that you complete and review often.

Conclusion

In this journey through the chapters of "Beyond the Ordinary Leadership, A No-Suck Leadership Manifesto", we have delved into the multifaceted realm of leadership, transcending the ordinary and embracing the extraordinary. Each chapter has been a stepping stone toward becoming an extraordinary leader, from defining diverse leadership styles to exploring the extra effort required for exceptional leadership, setting ambitious goals, and embracing accountability.

The dynamics of leading, mentoring, coaching, and managing have been thoroughly examined, along with strategies to harmonize work and life, avoiding burnout in the pursuit of no-suck leadership. As we reflect on what constitutes a leadership legacy and the importance of self-care and continuous personal growth, the guide provides a thought-provoking exploration of "Things that make you go hmmm." This chapter was filled with great examples of leadership faux paus. The following appendices will provide you with practical tools such as Lindsay's Quick Tips for Successful Leadership and a Personalized Learning Plan Template.

As we reach the end, I hope this book has expanded your understanding of leadership and ignited a spark to go beyond the ordinary in your leadership journey. Remember, the extraordinary is not a destination but a continuous evolution, and your leadership legacy is shaped by the intentional choices you make every day. May your leadership path be fulfilling and impactful as you strive for greatness in every aspect of your life. Never stop learning, teaching, and growing.

Appendix

Appendix A: Lindsay's Quick No-Suck Tips for Success

- Leaders are always willing to jump in and help.
- A good leader helps develop their team by providing resources and guidance rather than doing their jobs.
- Good leaders understand when to call it quits for the day and do not value working excessively.
- While it's possible to excel as a parent, friend, spouse, and leader, it is crucial to prioritize appropriately. Fully commit to your role as a leader during work hours, and once you're home, focus on being present with your friends and loved ones and yourself, leaving work-related concerns at the workplace.
- Demonstrate the values and work ethic you expect from your team. Your actions set the standard for others to follow.
- Foster positive relationships with team members. Understand their strengths, weaknesses, and aspirations. A strong team is built on trust and mutual respect.
- Understand and consider the feelings and perspectives of your team members. Show empathy and be supportive, especially during challenging times.

- Foster a creative and innovative environment. Encourage team members to share ideas and take calculated risks.
- Trust your team members with responsibilities that align with their strengths. Delegating tasks empowers individuals and allows you to focus on strategic aspects of leadership.
- Think ahead and plan strategically. Anticipate challenges and proactively address them to keep the team on the path to success.
- Recognize and appreciate the efforts of your team. Regularly acknowledge accomplishments, both big and small, to boost morale.
- Demonstrate resilience and maintain composure during challenging situations. Your ability to stay calm can inspire confidence in your team.
- Offer feedback that is specific, constructive, and actionable. Acknowledge achievements and provide guidance on areas for improvement.
- Be flexible and able to adapt to changing circumstances. A great leader can navigate through uncertainties and lead the team to success.
- Support the growth and development of your team members. Provide opportunities for training and skill-building to enhance their professional capabilities.

Appendix B. Personalized Learning Plan Template
Current Skills Assessment
1. **Strengths**
   a. List your current strengths.
2. **Areas of Opportunity**
   b. Identify the areas where you need/want to enhance your skills.

    c. Identify new skills you want to acquire.

Learning Goals
Short-Term Goals (1-3 Months)
1. Goal 1:
   a. Objective or Skill you want to achieve.
   b. What actions need to be taken to achieve this goal?
   c. What tools, materials, and courses will you need?
2. Goal 2:
   a. Objective or Skill you want to achieve.
   b. What actions need to be taken to achieve this goal?
   c. What tools, materials, and courses will you need?

Mid-Term Goals (3-6 Months)
3. Goal 3:
   a. Objective or Skill you want to achieve.
   b. What actions need to be taken to achieve this goal?
   c. What tools, materials, and courses will you need?
4. Goal 4:
   a. Objective or Skill you want to achieve.
   b. What actions need to be taken to achieve this goal?
   c. What tools, materials, and courses will you need?

Long-Term Goals (1 Year)
5. Goal 5:
   a. Objective or Skill you want to achieve.
   b. What actions need to be taken to achieve this goal?
   c. What tools, materials, and courses will you need?
6. Goal 6:
   a. Objective or Skill you want to achieve
   b. What actions need to be taken to achieve this goal?
   c. What tools, materials, and courses will you need?

Progress
1. Metrics for Success
   a. How will you measure your progress? (Set milestones and specific metrics.)
2. Timeline
   b. Set a timeline for each goal and the associated action steps.

Reflection and Revision
1. Reflection
   a. Schedule a weekly time to reflect on your progress and challenges and notate.
2. Revision
   a. After reflecting, what revisions need to be made, if any.

Support Network
1. Mentors/Peers
   a. List the people who can provide guidance and support.
2. Courses/Workshops
   a. List relevant courses that will contribute to your development and goal completion.
3. Books/Articles
   a. List all recommended reading materials.

Commitment Pledge
I, (Your Name), am committed to following my personalized learning plan to achieve my development goals. I understand the importance of self-improvement in reaching my full potential.

Signature:

Date:

Appendix C. Vision Boards
Examples:

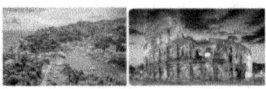
2025 Vision Board

Travel - 2025 Italy

Health - Join the gym and take 3 Fitness Classes Per week

Finances - Purchase an Invest Home and Open a 401K

Family - Implement Technology free dinners

Template Example:

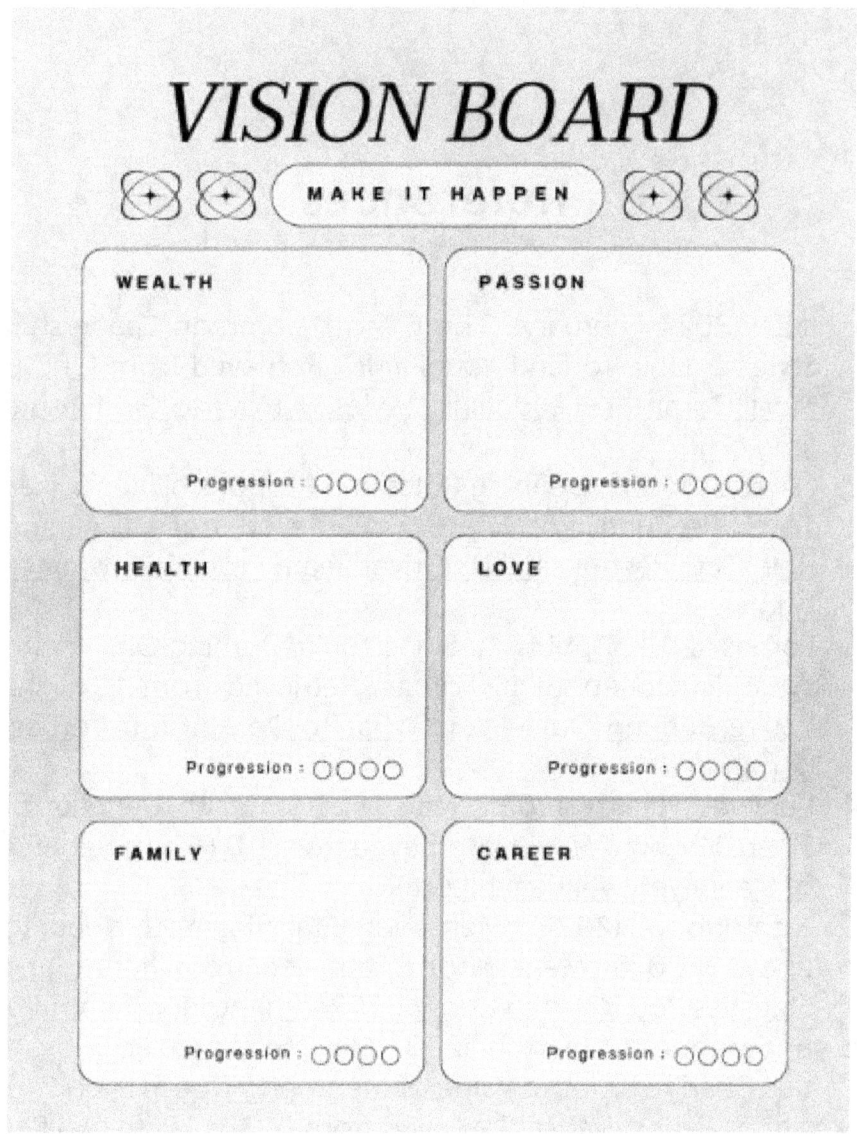

References

1. IMD. (2024 February). The 6 Most Common Leadership Styles & How to Find Yours. *IMD*. Retrieved from [The 6 Most Common Leadership Styles & How to Find Yours (imd.org)]
2. Ninety.io. (n.d.). Defining Roles and Responsibilities Drives Team Productivity. *Ninety.io*. Retrieved from [Defining Roles and Responsibilities Drives Team Productivity (ninety.io)]
3. Forbes. (2013, April 1). 10 Signs You're Burning Out -- And What To Do About It. *Forbes*. Retrieved from 10 Signs You're Burning Out -- And What To Do About It (forbes.com)]
4. Verywell Health. (2023, May 18). 10 Health Benefits of Sleep. *Verywell Health*. Retrieved from [10 Health Benefits of Sleep (verywellhealth.com)]
5. Mentorloop. (2024). Mentoring Statistics You Need to Know - 2023. *Mentorloop*. Retrieved from [Mentoring Statistics You Need to Know - 2024 (mentorloop.com)]
6. Knowledge at Wharton. (2007, May 16). Workplace Loyalties Change, but the Value of Mentoring Doesn't. *University of Pennsylvania*. Retrieved from [Workplace Loyalties Change, but the Value of Mentoring Doesn't - Knowledge at Wharton (upenn.edu)]
7. Guider AI. (2024). Mentoring Statistics For 2024. *Guider AI*. Retrieved from [Mentoring Statistics For 2024 | Guider AI (guider-ai.com)]

8. Forbes. (2024) A Psychologist Explains The Power Of 'Vision Boarding' For Success. Retrieved from <u>A Psychologist Explains The Power Of 'Vision Boarding' For Success (forbes.com)</u>

Testimonials

Lindsay has taught me so much about what it takes to be a good leader. She empowers and inspires her employees to excel & thrive in their positions. I am so grateful for all that she has taught me.
Jessica Bargenquast, Marketing Manager

Lindsay is one of those stellar bosses that you will ALWAYS compare to everyone else. She believes in lifting her people, setting clear achievable goals, and making sure you have the tools and resources for continued growth. If you are looking for sound advice on tuning up your management skills, you've arrived at the right place and, the right person!
Mindy Drexler, Senior Product Marketing Manager

During my time working under Lindsay's leadership, I had the privilege of getting to know her closely. It was truly inspiring to work with such a great boss, who trusted, empowered and supported her team. Lindsay's open-mindedness and willingness to embrace new ideas created a dynamic and collaborative environment. She not only encouraged my professional growth but also facilitated it by allowing me to shadow her and providing invaluable mentorship even after our professional path diverged. Lindsay is such an incredible leader and I am grateful for the lessons learned and the friendship developed.
Avery Hayden, Marketing Director

Lindsay has a great leadership balance being both assertive and empathetic. She leads by example and cultivates extreme loyalty within her team. Her leadership abilities are top notch.
Sean McGraw, CEO

www.ingramcontent.com/pod-product-compliance
Lightning Source LLC
LaVergne TN
LVHW012026060526
838201LV00061B/4489